Easy Wine Making
in 21 days

John George and Barrie Anderson

HAMLYN
London · New York · Sydney · Toronto

Contents

Illustrated by Tony Streek

Jacket photograph by Iain Reid

Published by
The Hamlyn Publishing Group Limited
London · New York · Sydney · Toronto
Astronaut House, Feltham, Middlesex, England
©Copyright The Hamlyn Publishing Group Limited 1976

Fourth impression 1979

ISBN 0 600 33115 6

Printed and bound in Great Britain by
Morrison & Gibb Ltd, London and Edinburgh

Do's
and don'ts

Remember that wine is not for swigging. It should complement the meal and be enjoyed as an integral part of the meal. The lighter the meal, the lighter the wine. If you just want a swig, then don't order, or make, a bottle of wine. Order, or make a pint of bitter.

Here's a list of do's and don'ts of wine making:

Do give special attention to sterilisation.

Do aerate the must during the first few days of fermentation to encourage development of the yeast colony.

Do decide at the outset the type and alcohol strength required.

Do try to understand the basic principles in each stage of your wine making.

Do try to maintain the temperature at a level of 75°F. (24°C.). A difference of 5°F. (3°C.) either way will not be detrimental.

Do keep jars topped up.

Do store finished wines in a cool place – between 45–50°F. (4–7°C.) if possible.

Do use parallel corks if laying wines down for storage.

Do chill white and rosé wines before serving, or before tasting for adjustment.

Do sulphite wines for long storage and maturing.

Do drink and enjoy your wines *when they suit your palate*, irrespective of their age.

Do not disturb a happily fermenting wine after the first racking.

Do not store your wine in polythene containers. Always use glass when available.

Do not over-filter or over-fine your wines.

Do not sell your wines. There is no restriction on the quantity you may make, *but under no circumstances must a single drop be sold.*

A new look
at an ancient craft

The field of amateur wine making has altered greatly during the past few years. Even 15 years ago the wine producing methods given in this book would not have been accepted. However, within the past five years a more than tolerant climate has emerged. Because amateur wine makers in this country have become more sophisticated, so home wine making has moved excitingly into the future. What has brought about this change? Education, through wine making clubs. In recent years, wine making clubs have become widely popular in Britain. They serve mainly as a social outlet, but they are also a means of helping the serious minded wine makers to come into contact with people of similar interests. Most clubs hold regular monthly meetings at which the members listen to a speaker, or see instructional films on wine making. The members are encouraged to discuss their mutual problems and are also able to sample other members' wines. More and more wine club parties are going on vineyard tours of France and, after sampling French wines, its members are realising that the wines are not like the carrot wine they have been used to making, and it dawns on them that what they have been producing at their clubs is very different from what they sample. For the truth is you cannot go to France and sample carrot wine because there is no such thing in France.

So, a new trend is taking place in the wine making field, and amongst its drinkers. They are demanding a higher standard from their products and there is a drift away from the once-accepted country wines. The amazing point is that it is far easier, today, to produce a high quality wine from concentrates, than it is to produce a so-called country wine which takes years to mature before it can be drunk.

The making of wine in Britain has been legal practice since early times and there is no doubt that some good wines have been produced. But, as with all other crafts there was little scientific knowledge available and there was a fair proportion of inferior or spoilt wines in the annual vintage. Wine makers had little idea of how to control the juice extraction and fermentation so as to ensure a sound disorder-free wine.

Similarly, there was little selectivity in the choice of ingredients. Many wines were initially very unpalatable and needed to be stored for some years before they became acceptable – the poor flavour having disappeared as other constituents in the wine blended together. Some ingredients created hazes in the wines which never clarified, for the early wine makers did not appreciate that some ingredients remained incapable of being fermented until they were reacted upon by substances known as enzymes.

If commercial wine makers remain patient people, amateur wine makers are increasingly not so. No longer are they prepared to wait several years for the wine to develop. They are beginning to realise that wines with disorders will become even more unpalatable, or that with adjustment of the constituents, wines can be made suitable for drinking within a few weeks.

By following our method, described in this book, which uses fruit and fruit concentrates or grape concentrate, sugar and additives, you can produce a high quality, simulated commercial wine which is drinkable, is equal to, and in some cases better than, the commercial product – within the space of three weeks.

At this stage in the book there will be perhaps some who will be sceptical that wine making can be learned from a book, considering, rightly, that the appreciation of wine is a practical act as it involves the use of the eyes, nose and palate. This line of reasoning is undoubtedly correct but it must be remembered that wine making is both an art – which is a practical subject – and also a science – which is a theoretical subject.

So, without fully understanding the basic principles of wine making there is always the possibility that problems of some sort will arise during the making of the wine. All disorders in wines result from lack of knowledge – nothing more. This does not mean that the wine maker needs to be a scientist in order to produce sound wines, but it does mean that basic principles should be understood and used. Therefore an hour or so spent in understanding the basic rules may save hours of wasted time and gallons of wasted wine!

Books on the market tend to tell the beginner that all wines are worth keeping – that the longer you keep a wine the better it will be. That appears as a very simple 'get out', and offers little comfort to the poor home wine maker who has just produced five gallons of wine only to find that he has to wait 18 months to two years for his wine to be palatable.

Admittedly, country wines do improve with keeping, provided that the acid and tannin balance is correct at the time of storage, but it is a great fallacy, accepted by a lot of people in the wine world, that all wines improve with keeping.

Our method of wine making has been proved by the successes in shows at county and national level. There have been instances where two- or three-week old wines were competing against wines from five to seven years old. In some cases this has been achieved by wine makers with only twelve months' experience, some with even less.

Wine can give enjoyment to the healthy, as well as benefit the ailing. Wine has something to offer everyone. The wines we hope you will make are designed to be drunk with a meal at one bottle per sitting. However, if the whole bottle is not consumed, and provided the remainder is firmly corked, your wine will still be drinkable up to seven days later.

Another advantage of wine making in three weeks is the saving of space. If wine took up to two years before anyone could drink it and if you were a regular bottle-a-day drinker you would need about 600 bottles stacked away in a massive cellar before you could even start drinking! With the trends today in house building, people living in high-rise flats and maisonettes, where is the space to store wine for 18 months or more?

With the method described, two five-gallon (22½-litre) containers, one of red wine and one of white wine, and, at the most, six square feet (½ square metre) of storage space is all you need.

There are various types of wine maker in the country. Some people who make wine do so because they want cheap alcohol and a drink. Other people make wine because they like wine to drink with their meals and commercial wine is becoming too expensive. In the old days we were paying the true value for what we were purchasing. Today we are not. For it can be substantiated that the standard of commercial wine is dropping; therefore if you can make a simulated quality wine at way below the cost price in the shops and produce a wine that suits your palate, you will not only be saving yourself some money but have an absorbing hobby as well.

Think in terms of the cheapest wine one can possibly buy in the commercial field today. Obviously it won't be a top quality wine, but it is the sort of wine which is passable with a meal. You feel you have had a drink when you have drunk it, but as a beginner are you to know you are drinking a low standard wine as compared with a quality wine? Though we all know the wine drinker who, as well as liking the palate taste, also likes to be able to say, 'I bought this – it cost so many pounds'. Be much more proud to tell your guests that you have made the wine and how little it has cost. Provided the wine is of a good quality – which it will be if you follow the recipes given and know the taste you're after – your guests will not be offended, but impressed, particularly if they compliment you on the excellence of the wine before you tell them the truth!

Unless one is a connoisseur, to pay large sums of money for wine is throwing away money. It is better to buy a bottle of wine in the lower price range, although even in this bracket one cannot afford to drink a bottle with one's dinner every evening of the year.

What are some of the differences between the fruit concentrate, simulated, commercial-type wines we are suggesting you make, and the home produced, country wines we have all come to know, made from carrots, potatoes, parsnips and turnips, and a wide variety of fruit and flowers?

Straight away we should be able to appreciate that country wines are not true wines. They are alcoholic beverages, solely alcoholic fruit juices which are often over-flavoured and over-strong. All root vegetables are starchy and often wines made from root vegetables can be very difficult to clear. The constituents in a wine consist of six main substances – alcohol, acids, tannin, sugar, flavour and body.

Some books on wine making say that a Sauternes-type wine can be made from root vegetables. Sauternes is definitely made from the grape and the aim of every wine maker should be to try and imitate the genuine product. You cannot hope to produce quality white wine (which is made from the grape) from potatoes, or red wine from beetroots! The presence of starch is not permissible in true wine since the by-product of starch produces the wrong type of alcohol.

Because country wines are purely and simply alcoholic fruit juices, after two or three glasses one has had sufficient. Often the alcohol level as well as flavour is far too high to be enjoyed and appreciated. Unfortunately this is due, in part, to the recipes recommended in some wine making books on the market today.

The genuine wine drinker who likes to enjoy a bottle of wine in the evening prefers to come down to a reasonable alcoholic level. A bottle of chilled wine placed on the table with a chicken salad, or a red wine served at room temperature with a meal, as a complement to that meal, should not have a higher alcohol level than the commercial counterpart. Your guests want to enjoy their evening and still be able to drive home afterwards.

So the first thing one has to do is to cut down the alcohol content of these country-type wines so that one can drink a bottle and enjoy it without any adverse effects. Study the hydrometer chart (which is shown on page 17, and carefully explained) for alcoholic strength, i.e. just how much sugar is needed to convert into 'x' amount of alcohol for, say, a table wine. We are not saying that fruit concentrate wines or the methods and advice given in this book produce wines which are better than the old country-style wines but do hope that the difference between country and commercial wine types will be appreciated, having carried out the recommended experiments and methods.

Here is a test: pour a glass of commercial wine of your choice into one of two identical glasses and then pour the simulation of that wine into the other glass. Then get a taster to close his eyes while you switch the glasses round a few times. The chances are he will not be too certain, if at all, which is the commercial wine. And when you taste you will be just as perplexed!

You may wish to simulate a commercial wine and want to know the taste. Don't buy a bottle of wine at a rock bottom price when the cheapest reasonable one your wine merchant will have will probably cost twice or three times as much. It should therefore be quite obvious it is not quality wine you are buying at the cheaper price, but in all probability a blend of wines, giving that wine a bad name.

The laws of wine are not to protect the consumer. They are introduced to protect the producer; therefore if some wines are getting a bad name simply because merchants are blending wines of a lesser quality with it, then it's the producers who have a right to get up in arms, not the drinker, who accepts that what he bought is genuine value for money.

The first task is for you, the wine maker, to make a basic wine which is of the same colour as the type you wish to simulate. The colour in a wine is determined by the colour of the flesh or juice of the ingredient. Some red-skinned fruits, for example, have yellow flesh and the resultant wine is white or golden. Leaving the skins in the must during the fermentation will cause colour changes – to some degree – and this technique is used by the commercial producers in the making of red and rosé wines.

Once you know what you like you will see that the recipes in this book show the fruit concentrate and additives suitable to produce *that* type of wine. It is then purely a matter of adjusting the balance – alcohol content, acid content and tannin to simulate the wine of your choice.

Climatic conditions decide how much acid is left in the fruit at the end of the season. In a warm climate the acids are converted to sugar, hence a sweeter wine. Conversely, go further north where the climate is cooler, the acids are not converted into sugar, then there is much more residual acid which produces a dry, sharp wine.

A hock wine for example has a preponderance of malic and tartaric acids in its early life, which after six to nine months and after the sugar fermentation is completed, cause a malo-lactic fermentation (sometimes known as sympathetic fermentation) and this converts the remaining raw acids into a softer, lactic acid. This accounts for the particular flavour of hock-type wines. Appreciate this and one can adjust a wine with a particular acid to produce a particular wine type. Therefore one can tailor-make a wine which is enjoyable and refreshing.

Appreciation and assessment begins when the fermentation process or conversion of the sugar is complete and the art of simulating wine therefore is in the understanding of the qualities expected in the finished product and in adjusting or blending to achieve the desired result. This is as true of the commercial product as it is necessary with the simulated one because one cannot guarantee a specific end result from a given fixed recipe. Vintners cannot guarantee that a vineyard's given production for one year is going to turn out the same as the previous year, because that year may have been a vintage year due, perhaps, to a good summer. The next year they may have had hailstorms and little sun, resulting in no ripeness to the grapes. In spite of the elements, the commercial wine maker must produce a good quality wine.

The method we employ, using fruit, fruit concentrates, sugar and additives, is not dependent on a good harvest. But as we are out to make sound, basic wines with clean bouquet and taste, the art of blending and adjustment must be learnt. All good wines have a common denominator – balance, the hallmark expected by the knowledgeable.

One does not necessarily have to imitate commercial wine to type to be considered a good wine maker. But to practise along these guide lines is the surest and quickest way to understand the all-important factors of wine making – the achievement of balance.

Basically, the art of the wine maker lies in being able to sustain the wine at a peak condition before it reverts to simpler forms, such as vinegar. Wine is an organic substance which means that it is capable of change and for this reason it needs care and attention throughout its life. The best way to this end is to drink it and enjoy it daily and not allow time to encourage its deterioration.

You should now be wanting to make wine by the methods described in this book. So we will not detain you longer, except to offer you this caution:

Do not make the mistake of many amateur wine makers today who think they can produce better wines than the professional. One can be considered a good wine maker when able to produce a wine to an accepted standard, and that is what we hope you will be able to do.

10

The basic recipe and method

You will probably have much of the basic equipment needed for wine making in the kitchen cupboard. However, we feel you should purchase a new set of equipment and keep it solely for wine making.

The initial outlay on equipment, ingredients, etc. need not be expensive. It should provide sufficient additives to last for the first few months, but naturally this depends on the amount of wine which is made. Most of the subsequent outlay is for the purchase of sugar, and basic ingredients. The sugar is essential for the production of alcohol, and the flavouring ingredients enable you to make a variety of wines. Dried ingredients vary less in price throughout the year, so for this reason they may be preferable to fresh fruits – except when the fresh fruit is in season and therefore less expensive.

You will need

A *plastic fermentation bin or bucket with a lid.*

A *polythene container* capable of holding five gallons (22½ litres) of wine. This is easily obtainable at a modest cost.

A *nylon sieve* for straining the must.

A *length of tube* for siphoning – about 4 ft. 6 in. (1⅓ metres).

A *long-handled wooden or plastic spoon* which will reach to the bottom of the container.

A *bottle brush* is absolutely essential. A nylon brush is better than a bristle one which is likely to sag or flop.

Cotton wool This is needed at the filtering stage.

A *filter* Our method favours the use of Theorit grade 5 filtering material. If preferred, you can buy a Harris filter from your local suppliers, or a Southern Vineyards Vinbrite. The main advantage of the commercial filters is that while the filtering is going on you do not have to attend to them.

A *wide polythene funnel* Again this is for the filtering stage.

It is advisable to purchase a *hydrometer* for checking the gravity during the fermentation stage.

Corks Always use new flange corks, or parallel corks if long storage, i.e. laying the bottle down, is required and these like most of the items listed above can be obtained from your wine making suppliers.

A *corking tool* for ramming home the parallel corks.

Finally, you will require a minimum of 30 bottles for your first batch of wine, as six bottles are needed for each gallon (4½ litres).

To produce a simulated, commercial wine following the methods directed in this book is, as we have already stressed, extremely easy, for most wines stem from the basic recipe. This recipe is as follows:

BASIC RECIPE

To make 5 gallons (22½ litres) wine – for 1 gallon (4½ litres) divide the amounts by 5.

Variable factors (see recipes)

fruit	root or grain
fruit concentrates	flowers

Constant factors (hot stage)

10 lb. (4½ kg.) sugar for a light wine
12½ lb. (5½ kg.) sugar for a medium wine
15 lb. (7 kg.) sugar for a social wine
5 teaspoons citric acid

2½ teaspoons tartaric acid
5 nutrient tablets, or 2½ teaspoons nutrient salts
1¼ teaspoons grape tannin

Constant factors (cool stage)

pectic enzyme, as instructed by the manufacturer, for fruit wines
amylase for use with root or grain

1¼ teaspoons energiser
yeast, as instructed by the manufacturer

(Please note that throughout this book all spoon measures referred to are level.)

Variable factors

Fruit This is variable in that if you decide to make a muscat wine, for instance, you would need only 5 lb. (2½ kg.) of muscatel raisins to produce 5 gallons (22½ litres) of wine. But if you decided to make an apple wine – and we would recommend crab apples because of the acidity and astringency – you would need 35 lb. (16 kg.) of apples to produce 5 gallons (22½ litres).

Fruit concentrates How much you need to produce 5 gallons (22½ litres) of wine depends on the strength of the concentrate and this may vary from one manufacturer to another. The details will be on the packaging, so follow the manufacturer's recommendations.

Flowers (petals) See the section on wines made from flowers, page 43.

Constant factors

Sugar This is necessary for the production of alcohol and determines the final sweetness of wine. Just how much sugar is needed is dependent on whether you want to produce a light wine, a medium wine or a social wine. This can be gauged by looking at the hydrometer chart on page 17. We know it looks complicated at first sight but after reading the instructions you will find it quite simple to comprehend. Here are the approximate alcoholic strengths for each of the three wine categories referred to:

Light wine 8·5% to 10·5% achieved by using between 1 lb. 11 oz. ($\frac{3}{4}$ kg.) and 2 lb. (1 kg.) of sugar.

Medium wine Up to 12·7% achieved by using between 2 lb. (1 kg.) and 2$\frac{1}{2}$ lb. (1$\frac{1}{8}$ kg.) of sugar.

Social wine Between 14% and 15% achieved by using between 2$\frac{3}{4}$ lb. (1$\frac{1}{4}$ kg.) and 3 lb. (1$\frac{1}{2}$ kg.) of sugar.

Some books on wine making specify that the sugar be added in stages, and the reason given for this is that too much sugar at a time overwhelms the yeast and makes the situation, within the must itself, unpalatable to the yeast. However, we feel the total amount of sugar included at the outset obviates the risk of stuck fermentations and achieves speedier results.

Citric acid When we come to special types of wine made from the basic recipe we will deal with the special types of acid, but the amateur cannot go wrong with citric acid because during the fermentation process this natural acid is completely burned up, leaving the wine flat. By adding 5 teaspoons of citric acid to 5 gallons (22$\frac{1}{2}$ litres) of wine it ensures a sound primary fermentation, through inhibiting bacterial infection as bacteria do not like acid conditions.

Nutrients These natural mineral salts come in both tablet and salt form – and we recommend a blend of five – phosphates, ammonium salts, sulphates, cobalt and magnesium iron – which are available from home wine making suppliers. Nutrients, which are an essential requirement for healthy yeast growth and development throughout all stages of fermentation, are found within the earth and come up through the sap of fruit trees to feed the fruit.

Tannin Astringency in a wine is a term often confused or described as bitterness by the uninitiated. Red wines contain about four to five times the amount of tannin found in white wines due to the longer fermentation required on the skins to extract the colour. Lack of tannin in wine leaves the wine insipid. Excess of tannin creates harshness. The addition of tannin also aids in the prevention of protein haze and is necessary if the wine is intended for long storage.

We recommend the use of grape tannin. It is produced specifically for wine making and is extracted from the pips and stalks of the grape vine.

The hot stage

You will see from the basic recipe that sugar, acids, nutrients and tannin are all added at the hot stage. So what do we mean by the hot stage? This is the stage where the boiling water is poured over the prepared ingredients in the bucket; for example, place 5 lb. (2$\frac{1}{2}$ kg.) of chopped raisins in a polythene

container capable of holding 5 gallons (22½ litres) of wine; add 2 gallons (9 litres) of boiling water, the sugar and additives and stir until the sugar has dissolved.

The cool stage
When the sugar has dissolved add 2 gallons (9 litres) of cold water mixed with the pectic enzyme, energiser and wine yeast. The container is now covered with a lid and put in an airing cupboard, or warm place. Stir the pulp once a day for the first four days to oxygenate it and help to get the yeast working.
Pectic enzyme This should be used as instructed on the packet. The addition of pectic enzyme reduces the gums and pectins into usable sugars.
Energiser This is added to infuse energy into the yeast.
Yeast Some people do not consider it essential to add yeast. However, if a wine does ferment and a true wine yeast has not been added it works on a wild yeast and this is a chancy business – one could end up with spoiled wine.

It was Louis Pasteur who, having been commissioned by the French Government of the period to look into the problem of yeast, discovered that it was not the yeast itself which produced the alcohol but that the enzymes produced by the yeast cells, created the alcohol. He proved this by grinding yeast with sand which destroyed the yeast completely, but left the enzymes which were responsible for the fermentation.

The cool stage. This is the stage when the pectic enzyme, energiser and wine yeast are added to the container; the container is then covered and left in a warm place for one week.

Fermentation
to bottling

There is quite a lot of information to be absorbed in this chapter but we will try to keep it as simple as possible. A week has passed and 5 gallons (22½ litres) of must, made to the basic recipe of 2½ lb. (1⅛ kg.) of sugar per gallon (4½ litres) – which should be ample for a table wine – has been fermenting merrily in a suitable place, disturbed only by the essential stirring for the first few days.

Now to work: you will need a 5-gallon (22½-litre) container – or five 1-gallon (4½-litre) containers. Glass is the best material for wine vessels, whether for fermentation or storage, because glass is chemically inert and not affected by the chemical constituents. Being transparent it is also easier to observe the progress of the fermentation and to see that the vessel is free from impurities which may affect the quality of the wine.

Scrub the containers thoroughly with a bottle brush dipped in hot water. Then rinse out each container in a solution of metabisulphate – 1 teaspoon to 1 pint (6 dl.) of water – to sterilise it.

Strain the liquid from the bucket through a nylon sieve into the 5-gallon (22½-litre) container, topping up to the neck with cooled, boiled water. Fit the air lock and put in a warm place about 75°F. (24°C.).

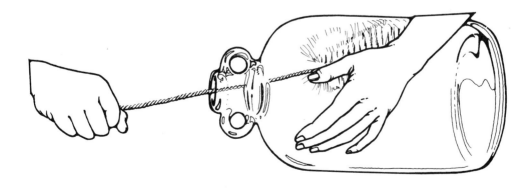

Scrubbing a container with a bottle brush dipped in hot water, ready for the strained liquid.

Air locks

There are several types of air lock available from home wine making suppliers. The plastic types are not so likely to get broken as the glass ones. The bubbler types are possibly better for the beginner as they indicate more easily the pressure of the carbon dioxide which is being expelled during fermentation. The function of the air lock is to allow the carbon dioxide to escape and also to prevent bacteria in the atmosphere reaching the fermenting must.

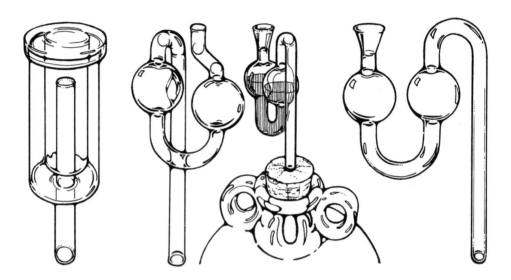

You are now left with a residue in the original container which you can throw on the compost heap. Thoroughly clean and sterilise this container and set it aside for future wine making.

After a further 7 days start checking the gravity of the wine with a hydrometer. Not everyone understands a hydrometer or hydrometer charts, so we will explain. A hydrometer is an instrument which is floated in a sample measure of liquid in a hydrometer test jar, to gauge the sugar content of the liquid. As the wine becomes more alcoholic the float sinks lower in the liquid. All you need to remember is that when the hydrometer sinks into the wine and reads 1000 showing at the liquid level, this is as far as you must allow it to fall, as it means the required gravity has been reached.

Now take a look at the hydrometer chart opposite. At first it may be confusing, but briefly what it tells us is this: that having started with a gravity of 1095 ($2\frac{1}{2}$ lb./$1\frac{1}{8}$ kg. sugar per gallon/$4\frac{1}{2}$ litres) and taking a reading after seven days we find it has dropped to, say, 1030. This means that the alcohol production to date is the original 12·7% potential of alcohol by volume *less* the achohol potential remaining which is 3·7%, which means that to date we have produced 9·0% of alcohol by volume.

Most wine books tell you to read the hydrometer chart from left to right. We say read it from right to left and only concern yourself with these two columns.

Hydrometer chart

Specific gravity	Amount of sugar (in lb. and oz.) in the gallon		Potential % alcohol by volume
1010		2	0·9
1015		4	1·6
1020		7	2·3
1025		9	3·0
1030		12	3·7
1035		15	4·4
1040	1	1	5·1
1045	1	3	5·8
1050	1	5	6·5
1055	1	7	7·2
1060	1	9	7·8
1065	1	11	8·6
1070	1	13	9·2
1075	1	15	9·9
1080	2	1	10·6
1085	2	4	11·3
1090	2	6	12·0
1095	2	8	12·7
1100	2	10	13·4
1105	2	12	14·1
1110	2	14	14·9
1115	3	0	15·6
1120	3	2	16·3
1125	3	4	17·0
1130	3	6	17·7
1135	3	8	18·4

We already know from the basic recipe that to produce a table wine, we need no more than 2½ lb. (1⅛ kg.) of sugar per gallon (4½ litres) of wine giving us a 12·7% alcohol content. But if you decide that you would be happier with 10·6% of alcohol present then, by looking up 10·6% on the hydrometer chart and reading across, you will see that all you need is 2 lb. 1 oz. (925 g.) of sugar in total per gallon to achieve this. And if subsequently you want to check the gravity you will see it to be 1080.

Taking an hydrometer reading.

Incidentally, if when you make a final reading, you find it has dropped below 1000 to say 995, again don't worry. You can bring it up to 1000 by the addition of sugar, if desired.

When your hydrometer is registering 1000 it means the liquid has become transformed into a more palatable substance. This is because the alcohol has a harmonising effect on the other constituents in the wine. This does not mean that the more alcohol which is produced the better the wine will be. The proportion of alcohol in the liquid should be directly related to the purpose for which the wine is intended – about 10% for table wines to about 16% or more for dessert wines.

Racking

This is the next stage to consider. Racking is the process whereby the liquid is siphoned off the sediment.

To rack the wine, place one end of the siphon tube into the wine in the container and suck on the other end to draw the wine along the tube. Holding

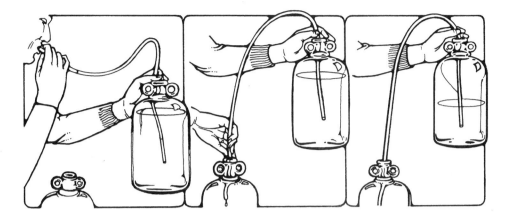

your finger over the end of the tube, place the tube in a sterilised receiving container, placed at a lower level than the one containing the wine. Remove your finger from the end of the tube and allow the wine to flow. Within 20 minutes or so you will have completed the racking process of 5 gallons (22½ litres) of wine and have a dry wine – because all the sugar has been consumed.

Although the wine has been racked it will still be in a murky condition and is still fermenting because the alcohol tolerance of the yeast has not yet been reached. We have produced a wine (because 2½ lb./1⅛ kg. sugar per gallon/ 4½ litres was used) with an alcohol content of 12·7%, but the alcohol tolerance of yeast working on the wine is about 16%. Therefore if fermentation is allowed to work without sugar the yeast will live on the body of the wine, so the fermentation has to be arrested. This is done by filtering the wine.

Filtering

To the racked wine add 2 crushed Campden tablets per gallon (4½ litres), to inhibit the yeast activity, and leave for 48 hours.

The debris, consisting of dead yeast cells and deteriorating pulp, which collects in the bottom of the container must not be allowed to remain because it may produce off-flavours in the wine. Also it is necessary to have the wine free from yeast flavours if the adjustment is to be carried out successfully.

There are many filtering devices available to the amateur wine maker and each is capable of polishing home-made wines to a very high standard. Our method of clearing wine is by the use of Theorit grade 5 filtering material. You will need the following equipment:
1 2-pint (generous 1-litre) jug
1 large funnel
1 wide-necked jar
1 roll non-medicated cotton wool
Theorit grade 5 filtering material

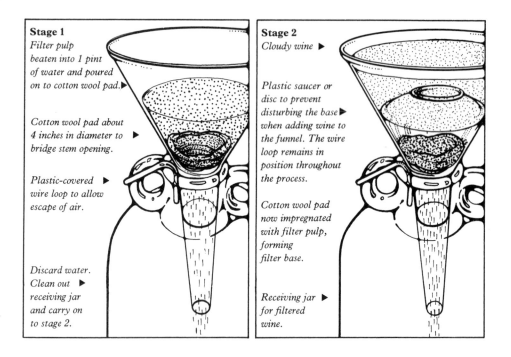

Stage 1

Filter pulp beaten into 1 pint of water and poured on to cotton wool pad. ▶

Cotton wool pad about 4 inches in diameter to ▶ *bridge stem opening.*

Plastic-covered ▶ *wire loop to allow escape of air.*

Discard water. Clean out ▶ *receiving jar and carry on to stage 2.*

Stage 2

Cloudy wine ▶

Plastic saucer or disc to prevent disturbing the base ▶ *when adding wine to the funnel. The wire loop remains in position throughout the process.*

Cotton wool pad now impregnated with filter pulp, forming filter base.

Receiving jar ▶ *for filtered wine.*

The funnel used for filtering should have most of the stem removed otherwise as the level of filtered wine rises in the receiving jar, pressure will build up in the stem and either stop the filtering or lift the filter bed thus allowing cloudy wine to seep into the wine already cleared. Before seating the funnel a loop of plastic-covered wire should be hung over the edge of the jar to allow the air to escape as it is being replaced by clear wine. Failure to do this can also stop the flow.

To form the filter bed Unroll a few inches of the cotton wool and cut out a piece approximately $4\frac{1}{2}$ inches (11 cm.) in diameter. Wet the funnel (this helps to hold the cotton wool in position) then place the cotton wool pad into the base of the funnel to cover the outlet. On no account should the pad of cotton wool be pushed into the stem of the funnel. Its purpose is to bridge the outlet and form a base for the pulp mixture.

Put 1 pint (6 dl.) cold water into a jug and add 1 heaped tablespoon of filter pulp, beat well, then pour this mix on to the cotton wool pad in the funnel and allow to settle. You will find that the pulp has sealed the edges of the pad and impregnated the cotton wool, thus creating a filter bed. Throw away the water which has filtered through and re-seat the funnel. To pour wine directly on to the filter bed would only disturb the filter bed; to prevent this, put a plastic saucer into the funnel, base up, and top the funnel up with wine, pouring on to the saucer, which is protecting the filter bed. The wine should now be entering the receiving jar, quite clear. Keep the funnel topped up as the greater the weight of wine the faster the filtration.

The purpose of filtering is to clean up the wine. As we have mentioned previously there are several methods of clearing wine but we recommend

Theorit grade 5, particularly as the wines we are making are designed to be consumed almost immediately.

If possible do try to filter your wines in the day time because you will be able to judge the clarity of your wines better by holding a sample glass to a north light where there are no reflections from the sun's rays which may obstruct your view of the wine.

Once true clarity is obtained with the first pint, proceed to filter the remainder; and if you don't want to filter all the remaining at one go add another Campden tablet or other stabiliser to each of the unfiltered gallons to avoid secondary fermentation taking place. This will also prevent oxidation.

Adjustment

Clearing a gallon ($4\frac{1}{2}$ litres) of wine may well take 45 minutes and once it is in a clear state, then, and only then, can you think about adjusting the wine. Never try to adjust fermenting wines. They may taste pleasant in the glass but, after filtering, the wine will have lost its yeast flavours and many of the fruit pulp flavours so you will not have had a true test of the intended flavour.

Look at your first clear gallon ($4\frac{1}{2}$ litres) of wine standing before you. The first thing to appreciate is that you have a wine already and you may decide that out of the six bottles one can fill from one gallon ($4\frac{1}{2}$ litres), two bottles should be corked as the wine stands because you've tasted it and like it. With the next two bottles why not experiment and produce a simulated commercial wine? For instance, an apple-based wine usually makes a good hock-type (see recipes on pages 26–27). So, secure in this knowledge, buy a half-bottle of hock to make comparisons.

The first thing you will notice about the apple wine is that it already has many of the qualities of hock, but there is a missing element, and that is the authentic bouquet. It has a nice bouquet but it is certainly not a hock bouquet. It has not the heavy scent of the living vine. If you have ever trodden on green vine leaves, or on a walk in a vineyard on a wet morning smelt the vine, it would be that bouquet you would be seeking in the hock.

Normally it would take nature up to two years to produce this bouquet which is how long it takes tartaric acid and malic acid to convert to lactic acid. We can achieve it in seconds, because we can add lactic acid, a few drops at a time until the desired result is achieved.

Assessing the quality of your wine

To adjust, first pour out half a glass of your apple wine and take a sip. Hold it in the mouth for just a few moments. Then open the mouth slightly and take in some air. Now swallow the wine and wait for the effects of the wine to come back. You can now give an assessment of that wine. It is probably rather mellow, rather bland. It is what we term a dumb wine: the alcohol is going round under the heat of the tongue but there is no bite. It is rather dull – proof that the wine is out of balance.

So, clear your palate with either a dry water biscuit or a piece of dry bread, for you can get a false impression on your next wine test if the previous taste is allowed to remain. Now take a second half-glass of the apple wine to which you have already added a drop or two of lactic acid, taste as you did before, and your mouth should begin to water because saliva is forming under the tongue and at the back. This is what a table wine should do – activate the taste buds, creating a saliva flow while you are eating, so that the enzymes produced in the saliva aid digestion.

Now take a third glass, this time of the commercial hock. Remember the taste you have just enjoyed, free your palate as before, then sample the commercial hock. It may be better, acidically, than your last taste, if so a little more lactic acid will be required in your simulation. How much? That you have to decide. But do it gradually.

You will probably make mistakes trying to get your simulations right, but that is the only way to learn. Even your mistakes should be drinkable and be enjoyable! Remember you still have another 4 gallons (18 litres) and two bottles of wine to experiment with.

Why not go for a Sauternes-type which is a sweet wine? Using the hock base you have already made, start adding sugar. A beginner may not know what a sweet wine is, so here is a way of learning to recognise a sweet wine. Pour water into four empty half-bottles. Put 1 teaspoon of sugar in one bottle, two in the next, three in the next, and four in the last bottle and shake each one until all the sugar is dissolved. When sipped they will all taste sweet. This is the same with wine, so we must look to the commercial standard which is recognised throughout the world, by investing in a half-bottle of good Sauternes. One of the sweetened half-bottles of water will be pretty near the real thing in sweetness, so you will have a measure to work to.

We feel that the medium-sweet Sauternes will be better than the very sweet because too much sugar will take away the beautiful acidic freshness. Over-sweetness becomes cloying which we consider unacceptable. So, as with the apple wine, and the hock-type, once you have achieved the taste you want, bottle the Sauternes-type.

Bottling

Good presentation is highly desirable. It is no good pouring out a well-filtered, well-adjusted wine, filled correctly to within $\frac{1}{2}$ inch (1 cm.) of the cork, if you present it badly. You can buy appropriate labels from your home wine making suppliers, and all wines should be labelled with the type, and date it was made. Wines should be put in the correct bottle – a hock has a long, tall, brown bottle while a Moselle comes in the same type of bottle, but a green one.

Out of your original 5 gallons (22½ litres) maybe you will want to set aside, say half, to mature for a special occasion. Bung in parallel corks and lay the bottles on their sides at an angle of less than 45° so that the air bubble remains at the top and the wine touches the cork and keeps it moist. But generally these wines are meant to be bottled and drunk young, allowing 7 days in the bottle to enable the wine to recover from the bottling process. Once your first 5 gallons (22½ litres) of white wine have been bottled and with the aid of the recipes on pages 38–41 we hope you will immediately be encouraged to make 5 gallons (22½ litres) of red wine from the basic recipe given.

Although the main object of this book is to help the beginner to produce a drinkable wine in 3 weeks, we recommend that, from time to time, you sample quality commercial wines, as this is an invaluable aid in the development of a palate. The choice of wines should be extensive – French, German, Spanish, Portuguese, Hungarian. In fact, as wide a range as possible. Once you are able to appreciate the balance of the constituents in the commercial wines, the easier it will be for you to adjust the young wines so that they become more palatable.

To summarise, here is, in brief, the full process:

Once you have made the basic recipe, ferment it for 7 days on pulp. Then strain and fit an air lock, making sure that the container is filled to the neck – top up with cooled, boiled water if necessary. Start checking the gravity, with the hydrometer, after a further 7 days. When the gravity reaches 1000, rack the wine and add 2 Campden tablets per gallon (4½ litres); after 48 hours, filter and adjust the acidity and sweetness to suit the palate.

Wine types - the use of various fruits for simulation

There are thousands of different types of wine produced throughout the world, and few people will have tasted them all. Fortunately, wines may be classified into groups and the differences between the wines in each group are of a very subtle nature. Not every wine maker likes all types of wines, so it is recommended that the beginner makes the types of wines which he is accustomed to drinking. For then there is a standard of commercial wine at which to aim.

What many people are not sure of is the names and classifications of wines within the categories. Firstly, let us look at the white wine section, ranging from light wines and progressing through to the more heavy-bodied ones.

White wines

Name of wine	Type of drink	Grade	Desirable alcohol by volume
Moselle	Table wine	Light	9·5%–10·5%
Hock	Table wine	Light to medium	10% –11·5%
Riesling	Table wine	Medium	10% –11·5%
Chablis	Table wine	Dry	11% –13%
Graves	Table wine	Medium-sweet	12% –14%
Sauternes	Table wine	Full-bodied sweet	12% –14%
Sweet muscat	Dessert wine	Full-bodied	12% –14%
Barsac	Dessert wine	Sweet (full-bodied)	12% –14%
Sauternes	Dessert wine	Full-bodied sweet	12% –15%

For the light table wines you should try to imitate the German, French or Portuguese wines. The advantage the home wine maker has is that he is able to produce a white wine from ingredients such as crab apples or cooking

24

apples which may be stored for use in the winter months. Elderberries and blackberries, which are the best basic fruits for making home-made red wine, are not so obliging. Therefore take advantage of specific fruits while they are in season.

In wine making, generally, correct acidity is essential and one garden fruit has the edge over others – the gooseberry. It is not called the 'hairy grape' for nothing. They actually have a combination of acids that perfectly imitate dry-type wines, for they contain both malic and tartaric acids, essential acids for German hock, light Moselle- and Riesling-type wines, though each has its own character obtained through a mineral salt balance. When using gooseberries it is advisable to ferment not less than 5 gallons (22½ litres), for you may well find you like it and since the gooseberry season is short you might miss out if you made only 1 gallon (4½ litres).

A good dried fruit to use is either sultanas or very light raisins. They are dried grapes, so by employing these you would be using the best ingredients. It is a matter of reconstituting the dried fruit with water, for all the mineral salts, sugar and tannins are still within the grape in its dried state.

Most German wines are drunk while they are young, and the lighter the wine the younger it should be consumed. A Moselle-type, for example, should be consumed within 12 months. Though young in our terms still means wine that can be enjoyed after one week of final clearing and adjusting. Always drink wines progressively, i.e. light – medium – full-bodied; dry – medium-sweet – sweet.

Fresh fruits, such as peaches and apricots, are best suited to produce the social wines rather than the table wines for one does not want these fruit flavours conflicting with the taste of one's food. So, basically the three fruits named, apples, gooseberries and sultanas, are the best ones to use for your simulated, white, table wines, dessert wines and social wines – sweet or dry.

Grapefruit, apricots and the quinces, all come into their own in white wines for their distinctive characteristic flavours.

RECIPES FOR WHITE WINES

To make 1 gallon (4½ litres) white, dry, light-bodied table wine (for 5 gallons/22½ litres multiply the amounts by 5)

Variable factors

3 lb. (1½ kg.) apples and ½ pint (3 dl.) grape concentrate or 8 oz. (225 g.) dried apricots and ½ pint (3 dl.) grape concentrate (or 8 oz./225 g.

light raisins) or 2 lb. (1 kg.) quinces and ½ pint (3 dl.) grape concentrate (or 8 oz./225 g. light raisins)

Constant factors (hot stage)

1 lb. 10 oz. (725 g.) granulated sugar
½ teaspoon nutrient salts or
  1 nutrient tablet

1 teaspoon citric acid
¼ teaspoon grape tannin

Constant factors (cool stage)

pectic enzyme, as instructed by the manufacturer

¼ teaspoon energiser
general purpose yeast

Wash and roughly chop the fruit and put into a clean sterilised polythene pail. Add the hot stage ingredients, then cover with 4 pints (2¼ litres) of boiling water. Stir until sugar has dissolved then add a further 3 pints (1½ litres) of cold water. Now add the cool stage ingredients and stir well. Cover the pail with a lid or a clean tea towel and leave in a warm place (about 75°F., 24°C.) for 7 days, stirring daily for the first 4 days. After the seventh day, strain the liquid into a 1-gallon (4½-litre) glass or plastic final fermentation vessel and fit an air lock. Keep the vessel in a warm place, making sure that the vessel is topped up to within 1 inch (2½ cm.) of the bung. Start checking the gravity after the fourteenth day from the start, and as soon as gravity reaches 1000 the wine will be ready for the next stage.

Irrespective of whether the wine is still fermenting, rack the wine from its present container into a clean, sterilised container and add 2 crushed Campden tablets. Leave for 24 hours, then filter. The wine can now be adjusted to simulate a commercial-type, or to suit your own palate.

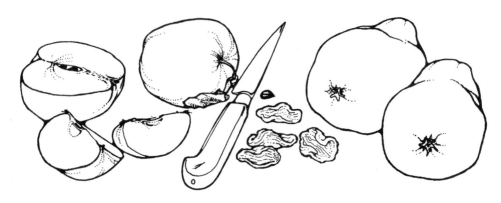

Types of wine you can simulate from this recipe

Moselles, Hocks, Rieslings and dry, white Burgundies.
Accompany Salads, fish dishes (particularly shellfish), chicken and poultry dishes and hors d'oeuvre.
Serve Chilled (40–45°F., 4–7°C.).
Type of glass Hock or a general Sauternes glass.

Graves-type wines – Sauternes, Barsac

Recipe As for a white, dry, light-bodied wine (see opposite), but with the addition of an extra ½ pint (3 dl.) of grape concentrate of an appropriate nature to impart extra body and flavour.
Method and procedure As for the white, dry, light-bodied table wine. Filter the wine at a gravity of 1000 and adjust to balance of a sample commercial wine, or to suit the palate.
Accompany Salads, fish dishes (particularly shellfish), chicken and poultry dishes and hors d'oeuvre.
Serve Chilled (40–45°F., 4–5°C.).
Type of glass A Sauternes-type glass. Treat as a beverage wine. Allow approximately half a bottle per person, with a meal.

Apricot or peach wines

These are white wines which merit both as table wines and as social wines.

Over-fruiting seems to be prevalent in some wine recipes which makes the finished wines taste as though one is eating the actual apricots which have been immersed in vodka.

Apricot wine, as opposed to alcoholic apricot juice, should resemble, and be described as a Sauternes-type wine with an overtone of apricot delicacy. This statement stresses the point that over-fruiting of wines destroys the delicate balance one would expect and appreciate in a wine of character. The following recipes will ensure wines worthy of presentation and appreciation, domestically and competitively.

APRICOT WINE 1

To make 1 gallon (4½ litres) light, dry table wine

8 oz. (225 g.) dried apricots or
  4 lb. (2 kg.) fresh apricots
1 lb. 10 oz. (725 g.) sugar
8 pints (4½ litres) water
1 teaspoon citric acid
½ teaspoon tartaric acid

1 teaspoon nutrient salts
¼ teaspoon tannin
¼ teaspoon energiser or 1 3-mg.
  vitamin B1 tablet
pectic enzyme
general purpose yeast

Chop or mince the fruit and place in a sterilised polythene pail (mark the 1-gallon/4½-litre level). Add the sugar and 4 pints (2¼ litres) boiling water and stir until the sugar has dissolved. Make up to 1 gallon (4½ litres) with cooled, boiled water, then add the rest of the ingredients – add the pectic enzyme and yeast according to the manufacturer's instructions. Stir well, then cover the pail with a lid or a clean tea towel and leave to stand in a warm place (70–75°F., 21–24°C.). Stir daily for the first 3 days to disperse the carbon dioxide and allow the yeast to develop. Allow the must to ferment for a further 4 days, then strain off the liquid into a 1-gallon (4½-litre) jar topping up with cooled, boiled water if necessary. Fit the air lock and return the jar to the warm place for further fermentation. Keep a close check on the gravity from now onwards as it has been known for the gravity to drop to 1000 within the first 7 days. When the gravity reaches 1000, or when dry to taste, rack off the wine into a second sterilised 1-gallon (4½-litre) jar. Add 2 crushed Campden tablets and allow to stand for 48 hours before fining or filtering.

After fining or filtering, adjust the wine for acidic or sugar balance to suit the palate. If acid adjustment is necessary, add 2 or 3 drops of lactic acid to suit taste.

To make *peach wine*, use peaches in place of apricots.

APRICOT WINE 2

To make 1 gallon (4½ litres) social wine

12 oz. (350 g.) dried apricots or
  6 lb. (3 kg.) fresh apricots
2 lb. (1 kg.) sugar
8 pints (4½ litres) water
1 teaspoon citric acid
½ teaspoon tartaric acid

1 teaspoon nutrient salts
¼ teaspoon tannin
¼ teaspoon energiser or 1 3-mg.
  vitamin B1 tablet
pectic enzyme
general purpose yeast

Chop or mince the fruit and place in a sterilised polythene pail (mark the 1-gallon/4½-litre level). Add the sugar and water and stir until the sugar has dissolved. Make up to 1 gallon (4½ litres) with cooled, boiled water, then add the rest of the ingredients – add the pectic enzyme and yeast according to the manufacturer's instructions. Stir well, then cover the pail with a lid or a clean tea towel and leave to stand in a warm place (70–75°F., 21–24°C.). Stir daily for the first 3 days to disperse the carbon dioxide and allow the yeast to develop. Allow the must to ferment for a further 4 days, then strain off the liquid into a 1-gallon (4½-litre) jar, topping up with cooled, boiled water if necessary. Fit the air lock and return the jar to the warm place for further fermentation. Keep a close check on the gravity from now onwards as it has been known for the gravity to drop to 1000 within the first 7 days. When the gravity reaches 1000, or when dry to taste, rack off the wine into a second sterilised 1-gallon (4½-litre) jar. Add 2 crushed Campden tablets and allow to stand for 48 hours before fining or filtering.

After fining or filtering, adjust the wine for acidic or sugar balance to suit the palate. If acid adjustment is necessary, add 2 or 3 drops of lactic acid to suit taste.

To make a *dessert wine*, use 1 lb. (450 g.) dried apricots or 8 lb. (3¾ kg.) fresh apricots and 2½ lb. (1⅛ kg.) sugar. Add 1 teaspoon glycerol per bottle after filtration and adjustment.

Gooseberry wine

For lovers of hocks, Moselles and Rieslings, the gooseberry is a must. For the dry, gay wines of the Moselle or Alsace and sparkling wines use the gooseberry when young and green and containing the natural acids so desirable in these wines.

GOOSEBERRY WINE 1

To make 1 gallon (4½ litres) Moselle-type wine

2 lb. (1 kg.) fresh green gooseberries
1 lb. 10 oz. (725 g.) sugar
8 pints (4½ litres) water
½ teaspoon citric acid
½ teaspoon tartaric acid
½ teaspoon malic acid

1 teaspoon nutrient salts
¼ teaspoon energiser or 1 3-mg. vitamin B1 tablet
¼ teaspoon tannin
pectic enzyme
champagne yeast

Crush the gooseberries well and place in a sterilised polythene pail (mark the 1-gallon/4½-litre level). Add the sugar and 4 pints (2¼ litres) boiling water and stir until the sugar has dissolved. Make up to 1 gallon (4½ litres) with cooled, boiled water, then add the rest of the ingredients – add the pectic enzyme and yeast according to the manufacturer's instructions. Stir well, then cover the pail with a lid or a clean tea towel and leave to stand in a warm place (70–75°F., 21–24°C.). Stir daily for the first 3 days to disperse the carbon dioxide and allow the yeast to develop. Allow the must to ferment for a further 4 days, then strain off the liquid into a 1-gallon (4½-litre) jar topping up with cooled, boiled water if necessary. Fit the air lock and return the jar to the warm place for further fermentation. Keep a close check on the gravity from now onwards as it has been known for the gravity to drop to 1000 within the first 7 days. When the gravity reaches 1000, or when dry to taste, rack off the wine into a second sterilised 1-gallon (4½-litre) jar. Add 2 crushed Campden tablets and allow to stand before fining or filtering.

After fining or filtering, adjust the wine for acidic or sugar balance to suit the palate. If acidic adjustment is necessary, add 2 or 3 drops of lactic acid to suit taste.

To make a *hock-type wine*, use 3 lb. (1½ kg.) gooseberries plus ½ pint (3 dl.) white grape concentrate.

GOOSEBERRY WINE 2

To make 1 gallon (4½ litres) social wine

4 lb. (2 kg.) ripe dessert gooseberries
2 lb. (1 kg.) sugar
8 pints (4½ litres) water
1 teaspoon citric acid
½ teaspoon tartaric acid
1 teaspoon nutrient salts

¼ teaspoon energiser or 1 3-mg.
  vitamin B1 tablet
¼ teaspoon tannin
pectic enzyme
general purpose yeast

Crush the gooseberries well and place in a sterilised polythene pail (mark the 1-gallon/4½-litre level). Add the sugar and 4 pints (2¼ litres) boiling water and stir until the sugar has dissolved. Make up to 1 gallon (4½ litres) with cooled, boiled water, then add the rest of the ingredients – add the pectic enzyme and yeast according to the manufacturer's instructions. Stir well, then cover the pail with a lid or a clean tea towel and leave to stand in a warm place (70–75°F., 21–24°C.). Stir daily for the first 3 days to disperse the carbon dioxide and allow the yeast to develop. Allow the must to ferment for a further 4 days, then strain off the liquid into a 1-gallon (4½-litre) jar topping up with cooled, boiled water if necessary. Fit the air lock and return the jar to the warm place for further fermentation. Keep a close check on the gravity from now onwards as it has been known for the gravity to drop to 1000 within the first 7 days. When the gravity reaches 1000, or when dry to taste, rack off the wine into a second sterilised 1-gallon (4½-litre) jar. Add 2 crushed Campden tablets and allow to stand before fining or filtering.

After fining or filtering, adjust the wine for acidic or sugar balance to suit the palate. If acidic adjustment is necessary, add 2 or 3 drops of lactic acid to suit taste.

To make a *dessert wine*, use 6 lb. (3 kg.) gooseberries and 2¼ lb. (1⅛ kg.) sugar.

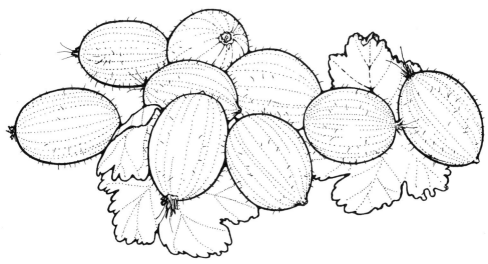

Raisin wine

The raisin and sultana are dried varieties of the grape and therefore among the finest of all dried fruits to use as a wine base in white wines. From experiments carried out over the past 15 years with different raisins, we recommend the following varieties to use for various wines:

Dry to medium light, table wine Thompson seedless
Social or dessert wine Valencia or Muscatel
Sherry-type wine Cyprus raisins
General purpose wine (Table/beverage/social/dessert) Australian Lexia raisins

Do not fall into the trap of thinking that the more fruit you use the better the wine will be. Good wine is a matter of balance and pleasant sensation imparted by the degree of balance, rather than an overpowering flavour of the fruit or basic ingredient used, plus a more than liberal lacing of alcohol. We have known of wines produced on as little as 1 lb. (450 g.) of raisins per gallon (4½ litres), which have won awards in table wine classes.

RAISIN WINE 1

To make 1 gallon (4½ litres) light, dry table wine

1 lb. (450 g.) light-coloured raisins
1 lb. 10 oz. (725 g.) sugar
8 pints (4½ litres) water
1 teaspoon citric acid
½ teaspoon tartaric acid
1 teaspoon nutrient salts

¼ teaspoon tannin
pectic enzyme
¼ teaspoon energiser or 1 3-mg. vitamin B1 tablet
general purpose yeast

Chop or mince the raisins and place in a sterilised polythene pail (mark the 1-gallon/4½-litre level). Add the sugar and water and stir until the sugar has dissolved. Make up to 1 gallon (4½ litres) with cooled, boiled water then add the rest of the ingredients – add the pectic enzyme and yeast according to the manufacturer's instructions. Stir well, then cover the pail with a lid or a clean tea towel and leave to stand in a warm place (70–75°F., 21–24°C.). Stir daily for the first 3 days to disperse the carbon dioxide and allow the yeast to develop. Allow to ferment for a further 4 days, then strain off the liquid into a 1-gallon (4½-litre) jar topping up with cooled, boiled water if necessary. Fit the air lock and return the jar to the warm place for further fermentation. Keep a close check on the gravity from now onwards as it has been known for the gravity to drop to 1000 within the first 7 days. When gravity reaches 1000, or when dry to taste, rack off the wine into a second sterilised 1-gallon (4½-litre) jar. Add 2 crushed Campden tablets and allow to stand for 48 hours before fining or filtering.

After fining or filtering, adjust the wine for acidic or sugar balance to suit the palate. If acid adjustment is necessary add 2 or 3 drops of lactic acid to suit taste.

The wine is now ready for drinking but will improve if allowed a resting period of a few weeks to absorb the oxygen introduced during the racking and filtering processes and to allow the acid and sugar used in balancing to marry.

This wine also produces a light sparkling wine using the method described for sparkling elderflower wine on page 47.

Try blending this wine with an equal amount of elderflower wine to produce a superb party wine.

To make a *medium wine*, use 2 lb. (1 kg.) sugar.

RAISIN WINE 2

To make 1 gallon (4½ litres) social wine

1¼ lb. (550 g.) raisins	¼ teaspoon tannin
2 lb. (1 kg.) sugar	pectic enzyme
8 pints (4½ litres) water	¼ teaspoon energiser or 1 3-mg.
1 teaspoon citric acid	vitamin B1 tablet
½ teaspoon tartaric acid	general purpose yeast
1 teaspoon nutrient salts	

Follow the method for raisin wine 1, but remember that fermentation will take longer as the higher amount of sugar will require a longer conversion period.

To smooth out the wine for immediate drinking, or to give the impression of maturity add 1 teaspoon of glycerol to each bottle. (Glycerol is obtainable from home wine making suppliers; alternatively use glycerine of BPC standard from the chemists.)

To make a *dessert wine*, use 2 lb. (1 kg.) raisins.

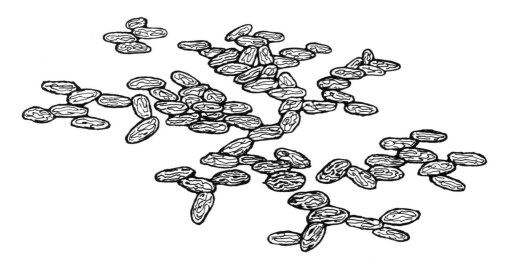

Rose hip wine

The rose hip is a very versatile berry capable of producing a variety of wine types and very useful to blend with both white and red wines. The range of colour can vary from pale straw to tawny depending on whether fresh or dried hips are used. Fresh hips will produce a wine of the Sauternes-type with the colour ranging from pale straw to gold, whilst dried hips or shells will produce wines of a sherry type ranging in colour from golden to tawny brown. The following recipes will produce sound, basic wines, well worth producing in their own right and certainly well worth experimenting with for blending.

ROSE HIP WINE 1

To make 1 gallon (4½ litres) light, table wine

2 lb. (1 kg.) fresh rose hips or
  8 oz. (225 g.) dried rose hips
enzyme (see method)
1 lb. 10 oz. (725 g.) sugar
½ pint (3 dl.) white grape concentrate
1 teaspoon citric acid
½ teaspoon tartaric acid

1 teaspoon nutrient salts
¼ teaspoon energiser or 1 3-mg.
  vitamin B1 tablet
¼ teaspoon tannin
pectic enzyme
general purpose yeast

Sterilise a polythene pail (mark the 1-gallon/4½-litre level) and put in the berries. Cover the berries with boiling water and when cool add the enzyme Rohament 'P' (obtainable from wine making suppliers). This degrades the cellular structure of the fruit allowing for better extraction of the juices and flavours. Macerate the fruit well and leave for 24 hours. Add the sugar, then make up to 1 gallon (4½ litres) with more boiling water. Stir well until the sugar has dissolved, then strain the liquid from the pulp into a second sterilised pail. Add the rest of the ingredients – add the pectic enzyme and yeast according to the manufacturer's instructions. Cover the pail with a lid or a clean tea towel and leave to stand in a warm place (about 75°F., 24°C.) for 3–4 days, stirring once daily. Transfer the fermenting liquid to a 1-gallon (4½-litre) jar and fit the air lock. If short of liquid to fill the jar, top up with cooled, boiled water to within 1 inch (2½ cm.) of the bung. Return to the warm place for further fermentation. When a gravity of 1000 has been reached, or the wine tastes dry, carry out the final fining or filtering, and if necessary adjust for acidic balance or sweetness; 2 or 3 drops of lactic acid will balance any lack of acid.

ROSE HIP WINE 2

To make 1 gallon (4½ litres) sherry-type wine

6 oz. (175 g.) dried rose hip shells or
  1 lb. (450 g.) whole dried hips
enzyme (see method)
2½ lb. (1⅛ kg.) sugar
4 oz. (100 g.) raisins (Valencia if
  obtainable)
1 teaspoon citric acid

1 teaspoon tartaric acid
1 teaspoon nutrient salts
¼ teaspoon energiser or 1 3-mg.
  vitamin B1 tablet
pectic enzyme
general purpose yeast

Sterilise a polythene pail (mark the 1-gallon/4½-litre level) and put in the berries. Cover the berries with boiling water and when cool add the enzyme Rohament 'P' (obtainable from wine making suppliers). This degrades the cellular structure of the fruit allowing for better extraction of the juices and flavours. Macerate the fruit well and leave for 24 hours. Add the sugar and raisins, then make up to 1 gallon (4½ litres) with more boiling water. Stir well until the sugar has dissolved, then strain the liquid from the pulp into a second sterilised pail. Add the rest of the ingredients – add the pectic enzyme and yeast according to the manufacturer's instructions. Cover the pail with a lid or a clean tea towel and leave to stand in a warm place (about 75°F., 24°C.) for 3–4 days, stirring once daily. Transfer the fermenting liquid to a 1-gallon (4½-litre) jar and fit the air lock. If short of liquid to fill the jar, top up with cooled, boiled water to within 1 inch (2½ cm.) of the bung. Return to the warm place for further fermentation.

When the gravity drops to 1000, feed the liquid with 3 tablespoons sugar syrup (made by dissolving sugar in water) at a time, until a total of 3 lb (1½ kg.) of sugar has been converted. When the final addition has been made and the gravity has reached 1000, carry out the fining or filtering.

Adjust the wine to suit the palate with the addition of 2 or 3 drops of lactic acid, if necessary, and add sugar to taste if the wine is too dry.

To each bottle of adjusted wine add a sherry glass of brandy to give the characteristics of sherry. (Polish spirit will *not* give the character required.) Allow 3 months for the marrying of adjusting additives, then surprise yourself and your friends with a wine we feel sure will become one of your standard productions.

Red wines

Here there is a greater range, allowing the blending of many more fruits.

Name of wine	Type of drink	Grade	Desirable alcohol by volume
Beaujolais	Table or social wine	Light fruity medium	10·5%–12·5%
Vin ordinaire	Table wine	Medium-bodied. Dry	11·5%–12%
Bordeaux/ clarets	Table wine	Medium to full-bodied. Dry	12% –14%
Burgundy	Table wine	Full-bodied. Dry	12% –14%
Rhône	Table wine	Full-bodied. Fruity. Dry (high alcohol content)	13% –16%

Obviously the most direct approach to the production of red wine types is to use the appropriate grape concentrates. These, and others, are available from stores specialising in home wine making supplies.

From the table above you will see that Bordeaux and clarets appear as one. This is because they are! Way back in the Middle Ages when Bordeaux belonged to England, regular shipments of wine from there were brought in. The wine arrived murky and was sold in that state in taverns, while those who could afford to store wine in cellars stored their casks to clear. Claret means clear wine, so the rich drank claret and the poor, Bordeaux!

The most suitable fruit for simulating Bordeaux/clarets, or any of the red wines, is the elderberry, for it has a great source of tannin, good colouring and imparts good body; it also has a good basic flavour and is comparable to many famous red wines.

Variable factors
3–4 lb. (1½–2 kg.) elderberries, blackberries, blackcurrants, raspberries or bilberries
½ pint (3 dl.) red grape concentrate
Constants As for the white wine recipes.
Method and procedure As for the white wine recipes.
Accompany Red meats, and savoury dishes.
Serve At room temperature (65–70°F., 17–21°C.).
Type of glass A claret glass, or more usually a Sauternes-type glass.

Simulation of the red, commercial types
We recommend you produce the red wines in their own right, i.e. elderberry, blackberry, etc., and achieve simulation by blending the finished wines.

To achieve a light, dry, red table wine – claret-type
Blend Two-thirds elderberry wine with one-third blackberry wine.
Accompany Red meats and game.
Serve At room temperature (70–75°F., 21–24°C.).
Type of glass A claret glass, or more usually a Sauternes-type glass.

Burgundy-type
Blend Two-thirds elderberry wine with one-third blackcurrant wine.
Accompany Red meats, game, stews, etc.
Serve At room temperature (70–75°F., 21–24°C.).
Type of glass A claret glass, or more usually a Sauternes-type glass.

Beaujolais-type
Blend Two-thirds blackberry wine with one-third elderberry wine.
Accompany Cold beef, ham or turkey.
Serve Cooled (45–50°F., 7–10°C.).
Type of glass A claret glass, or more usually a Sauternes-type glass.

Medium-bodied, red table wines
Recipe The same as for obtaining the other red wines, but increase the variable factors by ½ pint (3 dl.) of red grape concentrate.
Accompany Red meats, game, stews, etc.
Serve At room temperature (65–70°F., 17–21°C.).
Type of glass A claret glass, or more usually a Sauternes-type glass.

Full-bodied, red table wines
Recipe The same as for obtaining the other red wines, but increase the variable factors by half the amount of fruit.
Accompany Red meats and game.
Serve At room temperature (65–70°F., 17–21°C.).
Type of glass A claret glass, or more usually a Sauternes-type glass.

Recipes for red wines

The red wine recipes given present a challenge to the ambitious wine maker in producing wines of quality approaching the standard of commercial clarets, Burgundy, Bordeaux, Beaujolais and Rhône-type wines.

Basic quantities of the following red wines will ensure that simulation of the red wines can be undertaken. Apart from the challenge of simulation, each basic wine, in its own right, will be well worth the effort and cost expended on its production.

The basic red wines required for experimentation are as follows:

Elderberry (dried)   Blackberry
Elderberry (fresh)   Bilberry
Elderberry (concentrate)   Blackcurrant

We suggest the production of 1 gallon (4½ litres) of each of the above as straight, red, fruit wines. The blending of these will be an exercise in simulation, giving pleasure, and unending incentive to achieve recognition amongst your friends and judges of quality wines.

ELDERBERRY WINE

To make 1 gallon (4½ litres) red, full-bodied wine

8 oz. (225 g.) dried elderberries or
 2 lb. (1 kg.) fresh elderberries or
 ½ pint (3 dl.) elderberry concentrate
 and ½ pint (3 dl.) red grape
 concentrate
7 pints (3¾ litres) water
1 Campden tablet
2 lb. (1 kg.) sugar

1 teaspoon citric acid
½ teaspoon tartaric acid
1 teaspoon nutrient salts
¼ teaspoon tannin
¼ teaspoon energiser or 1 3-mg.
 vitamin B1 tablet
pectic enzyme
general purpose yeast

Put the fruit (or fruit concentrate) in a sterilised polythene pail. Bring 2 pints (generous litre) of the water to the boil and pour into the pail. Add the Campden tablet. Leave for 24 hours, then mash to a purée. Add the sugar and remaining water, boiling. Stir until the sugar has dissolved. When cool, strain into a second sterilised pail and add the remaining ingredients – add the pectic enzyme and yeast according to the manufacturer's instructions. Cover the pail with a lid or a clean cloth and leave to stand in a warm place (about 75°F., 24°C.) for 4 days, stirring the ingredients once a day.

Transfer to a 1-gallon (4½-litre) jar, topping up with cooled, boiled water if necessary. Fit the air lock and return to the warm place for further fermentation.

When the gravity has dropped to 1000, or the wine tastes dry, carry out the final filtering process. If necessary, adjust for acid balance with 2 or 3 drops of lactic acid, and adjust for sweetness to suit the palate.

BLACKBERRY WINE

To make 1 gallon (4½ litres) dry wine

4–6 lb. (2–3 kg.) ripe blackberries
½ pint (3 dl.) red grape concentrate
7 pints (3¾ litres) water
1 Campden tablet
2 lb. (1 kg.) sugar
1 teaspoon citric acid

½ teaspoon tartaric acid
1 teaspoon nutrient salts
¼ teaspoon energiser or 1 3-mg.
  vitamin B1 tablet
pectic enzyme
general purpose yeast

Put the blackberries and grape concentrate in a sterilised polythene pail. Bring 2 pints (generous litre) of the water to the boil and pour into the pail. Add the Campden tablet. Leave for 24 hours, then mash to a purée. Add the sugar and remaining water, boiling. Stir until the sugar has dissolved. When cool, strain into a second sterilised pail and add the remaining ingredients – add the pectic enzyme and yeast according to the manufacturer's instructions. Cover the pail with a lid or a clean cloth and leave to stand in a warm place (about 75°F., 24°C.) for 4 days, stirring the ingredients once a day.

Transfer to a 1-gallon (4½-litre) jar, topping up with cooled, boiled water if necessary. Fit the air lock and return to the warm place for further fermentation.

When the gravity has dropped to 1000, or the wine tastes dry, carry out the final filtering process. If necessary, adjust for acid balance with 2 or 3 drops of lactic acid, and adjust for sweetness to suit the palate.

BILBERRY WINE

To make 1 gallon (4½ litres) dry wine

4 oz. (100 g.) dried bilberries
½ pint (3 dl.) red grape concentrate
7 pints (3¾ litres) water
1 Campden tablet
2 lb. (1 kg.) sugar
1 teaspoon citric acid
½ teaspoon tartaric acid

1 teaspoon nutrient salts
¼ teaspoon tannin
¼ teaspoon energiser or 1 3-mg. vitamin B1 tablet
pectic enzyme
general purpose yeast

Put the bilberries and grape concentrate in a sterilised polythene pail. Bring 2 pints (generous litre) of the water to the boil and pour into the pail. Add the Campden tablet. Leave for 24 hours, then mash to a purée. Add the sugar and remaining water, boiling. Stir until the sugar has dissolved. When cool, strain into a second sterilised pail and add the remaining ingredients – add the pectic enzyme and yeast according to the manufacturer's instructions. Cover the pail with a lid or a clean cloth and leave to stand in a warm place (about 75°F., 24°C.) for 4 days, stirring the ingredients once a day.

Transfer to a 1-gallon (4½-litre) jar, topping up with cooled, boiled water if necessary. Fit the air lock and return to the warm place for further fermentation.

When the gravity has dropped to 1000, or the wine tastes dry, carry out the final filtering process. If necessary, adjust for acid balance with 2 or 3 drops of lactic acid, and adjust for sweetness to suit the palate.

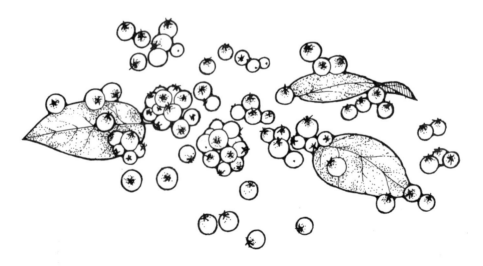

BLACKCURRANT WINE

To make 1 gallon (4½ litres)

4 lb. (2 kg.) ripe blackcurrants
½ pint (3 dl.) red grape concentrate
7 pints (3¾ litres) water
1 Campden tablet
2 lb. (1 kg.) sugar
1 teaspoon citric acid
½ teaspoon tartaric acid

1 teaspoon nutrient salts
¼ teaspoon tannin
¼ teaspoon energiser or 1 3-mg.
  vitamin B1 tablet
pectic enzyme
general purpose yeast

Put the blackcurrants and grape concentrate in a sterilised polythene pail. Bring 2 pints (generous litre) of the water to the boil and pour into the pail. Add the Campden tablet. Leave for 24 hours, then mash to a purée. Add the sugar and remaining water, boiling. Stir until the sugar has dissolved. When cool, strain into a second sterilised pail and add the remaining ingredients – add the pectic enzyme and yeast according to the manufacturer's instructions. Cover the pail with a lid or a clean cloth and leave to stand in a warm place (about 75°F., 24°C.) for 4 days, stirring the ingredients once a day.

Transfer to a 1-gallon (4½-litre) jar, topping up with cooled, boiled water if necessary. Fit the air lock and return to the warm place for further fermentation.

When the gravity has dropped to 1000, or the wine tastes dry, carry out the final filtering process. If necessary, adjust for acid balance with 2 or 3 drops of lactic acid, and adjust for sweetness to suit the palate.

Experiment in simulation

Having produced sound, basic dry red wines from the given recipes, rewarding results can be achieved by blending these wines.

Burgundy-type wine
Blend 1 bottle dry elderberry wine
        1 bottle dry bilberry wine
        1 bottle dry blackberry wine

Beaujolais-type wine
Blend 1 bottle dry elderberry wine
        2 bottles dry blackberry wine

Rhône-type wine
Blend 2 bottles dry elderberry wine
        1 bottle bilberry wine

To produce a social wine from any of these, add sugar to suit the palate.

Serving your wines

Having made quality wine, and as incorrect presentation may detract from your guests' enjoyment and full appreciation of your ability as a wine maker, references are made to the serving temperature, and with what food or on which occasions the wines would normally be served; the drawings below show the types of glass for the various wines – an important point as wine is enhanced by the glass in which it is served. Its visual aspect is the first impression, while clarity and colour are of immense importance. Balance plus colour, plus correct alcohol content ensures acceptance of the proffered glass.

Flower wines

Flower wines can be made from a wide variety of cultivated and wild flowers. They can be used with varying amounts of fruits, either as bouquet providers, or used on their own to produce delicate, light wines in their own right. We recommend the use of a small amount of grape concentrate or fruit as a body provider. Some of the popular flowers can be bought in dried form from home wine making suppliers or herbalists and only require infusion to extract the necessary flavour and bouquet.

The garden also provides a variety of flowers suitable for use in wine making and many popular varieties can be found in the hedgerows, on heaths and in woodlands.

The following recipes will guarantee successful wines.

Always gather flowers on a dry day, when the blooms are fully open, and at their best. Remember, that we want to extract from the blooms the flavour, bouquet and aroma contained in the volatile oils, and this can be easily over-done by using an excess of flowers, resulting in a good imitation of after-shave lotion! A flower wine should be light and delicate with an alcohol content of approximately 10–12%, and drunk slightly chilled.

Our method is to infuse the flowers, as in tea making, and strain off the liquid when sufficient colour and flavour has been extracted. About 1–2 hours is all the time required for this operation. The flowers should then be discarded, and never used in the must. If grape concentrate is used (which we recommend) to add body and vinosity to the wine, then the wine can go straight into the fermenting vessel for the fermentation period. This is a great advantage where space is a consideration.

If dried or fresh fruits are used as the body medium it will be necessary to ferment on the crushed or chopped pulp with the extracted infusion for 4–7 days before straining into the fermenting vessel.

When measuring the flowers, press them down lightly in the measure – do not pack them too tightly.

Dandelion wine

Dandelions grow wild in most parts of the world and are regarded as a weed. They flower from the end of April and through the summer. Use only the petals for making wine as any green parts can give the wine a bitter taste. Gather them on a dry, sunny day when the flowers are fully open as they provide homes for a host of insects when closed during dull, damp days.

Dandelions produce a Graves-type wine which should be served slightly chilled.

DANDELION WINE

To make 1 gallon (4½ litres) medium table wine

2 pints (generous litre) fresh flowers
  or 1 oz. (25 g.) dried flowers
7 pints (3¾ litres) water
1½ lb. (675 g.) sugar
1 pint (6 dl.) white grape concentrate
  or 1 lb. (450 g.) sultanas
1 teaspoon citric acid

½ teaspoon tartaric acid
1 teaspoon nutrient salts
¼ teaspoon energiser or 1 3-mg.
  vitamin B1 tablet
¼ teaspoon tannin
pectic enzyme (if using sultanas)
general purpose yeast

Put the flowers in a sterilised 2-gallon (9-litre) polythene pail and cover with 6 pints (3¼ litres) boiling water. Leave to infuse for 15–20 minutes, then strain off the extract into a second sterilised pail. Add the sugar and stir until dissolved. Add the grape concentrate or sultanas plus the remaining ingredients – add the pectic enzyme (if used) and the yeast according to the manufacturer's instructions. Cover the pail with a lid or a clean tea towel and leave in a warm place (about 75°F., 24°C.) to ferment, stirring once a day for the first 3 days.

After 3 days, transfer the fermenting liquid into a 1-gallon (4½-litre) jar (or other suitable container). If necessary, top the jar up with cooled, boiled water. If heavy frothing occurs after you have transferred the liquid to the jar allow it to subside before topping up. Fit the air lock and return the jar to the warm place for further fermentation.

After 14 days from the start, check the gravity with the hydrometer (or by tasting). If the wine has a gravity of 1000 (or is dry to taste), then the wine has achieved its alcohol potential. To allow the wine to ferment any further only reduces the balance which will create problems later on.

Rack the wine off the lees into a sterilised jar, add 2 crushed Campden tablets and leave for 48 hours. Filter the wine to remove any debris which may give it off-flavours.

After filtering, adjust the wine to suit the palate. If acidic adjustment is necessary, add 2 or 3 drops of lactic acid.

To make a *social wine*, use 2 lb. (1 kg.) sugar.

Coltsfoot wine

Coltsfoot can be found on wasteland and in country hedgerows and should be gathered during February. (The flowers appear well in advance of the leaf.) Use at the rate of 2–3 pints ($1\frac{1}{4}$–$1\frac{1}{2}$ litres) of fresh flowers per gallon ($4\frac{1}{2}$ litres), or 1–2 oz. (25–50 g.) of dried flowers.

Coltsfoot produces a Sauternes-type wine or social wine depending on the alcoholic strength. Serve slightly chilled.

COLTSFOOT WINE

To make 1 gallon ($4\frac{1}{2}$ litres) table wine

2 pints (generous litre) fresh flowers or 1 oz. (25 g.) dried
7 pints ($3\frac{3}{4}$ litres) water
$1\frac{1}{2}$ lb. (675 g.) sugar
$\frac{1}{2}$ pint (3 dl.) white grape concentrate or 8 oz. (225 g.) raisins, chopped
1 teaspoon nutrient salts

1 teaspoon citric acid
$\frac{1}{2}$ teaspoon tartaric acid
$\frac{1}{4}$ teaspoon tannin
$\frac{1}{4}$ teaspoon energiser or 1 3-mg. vitamin B1 tablet
pectic enzyme (if using raisins)
general purpose yeast

Put the flowers in a sterilised 2-gallon (9-litre) polythene pail and cover with boiling water. Leave to infuse for 15–20 minutes, then strain off the extract into a second sterilised pail. Add the sugar and stir until dissolved. Add the grape concentrate or raisins plus the remaining ingredients – add the pectic enzyme (if used) and the yeast according to the manufacturer's instructions. Cover the pail with a lid or a clean tea towel and leave in a warm place (about 75°F., 24°C.) to ferment, stirring once a day for the first 3 days.

After 3 days, transfer the fermenting liquid into a 1-gallon ($4\frac{1}{2}$-litre) jar (or other suitable container). If necessary, top the jar up with cooled, boiled water. If heavy frothing occurs after you have transferred the liquid to the jar allow it to subside before topping up. Fit the air lock and return the jar to the warm place for further fermentation.

After 14 days from the start, check the gravity with the hydrometer (or by tasting). If the wine has a gravity of 1000 (or is dry to taste), then the wine has achieved its alcohol potential. To allow the wine to ferment any further only reduces the balance which will create problems later on.

Rack the wine off the lees into a sterilised jar, add 2 crushed Campden tablets and leave for 48 hours. Filter the wine to remove any debris which may give it off-flavours.

After filtering, adjust the wine to suit the palate. If acidic adjustment is necessary, add 2 or 3 drops of lactic acid.

To make a *social wine*, use 3 pints ($1\frac{1}{2}$ litres) fresh flowers or 2 oz. (50 g.) dried flowers, 2 lb. (1 kg.) sugar and 1 pint (6 dl.) white grape concentrate or 1 lb. (450 g.) chopped raisins.

Elderflower wine

Elderflowers make one of the most beautiful flower wines when made correctly, and one of the most unpalatable when made incorrectly. Elderflower wine is regarded as the queen of wines so this particular recipe needs more detailed instructions – follow the instructions carefully.

Elderflowers grow in profusion in many parts of the world. They can be found in hedgerows and woodlands in the British Isles, but there are several varieties and collecting the wrong species of flower can produce a wine which could lose you many friends.

Only collect the flowers when they are in full bloom and fragrant – a guide to this is a pure white flower, fairly loosely packed on the stems. Always smell elderflowers before you pick them and gather only the flowers which have a pleasant scent. Avoid the closely packed, creamy-headed variety, which has an unpleasant smell. The florets should be removed from the stalks and infused as soon as possible after gathering, to capture the volatile oils and to prevent oxidation to which these flowers are prone.

Elderflowers can also be used to give a bouquet to other wines, but use them very sparingly. In a fruit wine, 2 teaspoons of dried elderflowers per gallon ($4\frac{1}{2}$ litres) will enhance the bouquet.

ELDERFLOWER WINE

To make 1 gallon ($4\frac{1}{2}$ litres) light, table wine

1 pint (6 dl.) fresh elderflowers
  or 1 oz. (25 g.) dried elderflowers
7 pints ($3\frac{3}{4}$ litres) water
$1\frac{1}{2}$ lb. (675 g.) sugar
$\frac{1}{2}$ pint (3 dl.) white grape
  concentrate (champagne or Riesling
  type)
$\frac{1}{2}$ teaspoon citric acid

$\frac{1}{2}$ teaspoon tartaric acid
$\frac{1}{2}$ teaspoon malic acid
1 teaspoon nutrient salts
$\frac{1}{4}$ teaspoon tannin
$\frac{1}{4}$ teaspoon energiser or 1 3-mg.
  vitamin B1 tablet
champagne yeast

Put the flowers in a sterilised 2-gallon (9-litre) polythene pail and cover with boiling water. Leave to infuse for 15–20 minutes, then strain off the extract into a second sterilised pail. Add the sugar and stir until dissolved. Add the grape concentrate plus the remaining ingredients – add the yeast according to the manufacturer's instructions. Cover the pail with a lid or a clean tea towel and leave in a warm place (about 75°F., 24°C.) to ferment, stirring once a day for the first 3 days.

After 3 days, transfer the fermenting liquid into a 1-gallon ($4\frac{1}{2}$-litre) jar (or other suitable container). If necessary, top the jar up with cooled, boiled water. If heavy frothing occurs after you have transferred the liquid to the jar allow it to subside before topping up. Fit the air lock and return the jar to the warm place for further fermentation.

After 14 days from the start, check the gravity with the hydrometer (or by tasting). If the wine has a gravity of 1000 (or is dry to taste), then the wine has achieved its alcohol potential. To allow the wine to ferment any further only reduces the balance which will create problems later on.

Rack the wine off the lees into a sterilised jar, add 2 crushed Campden tablets and leave for 48 hours. Filter the wine to remove any debris which may give it off-flavours. After filtering, adjust the wine to suit the palate. If acidic adjustment is necessary, add 2 or 3 drops of lactic acid.

To make a *social wine*, use 1¾ lb. (800 g.) sugar.

Sparkling-type wine

To produce a sparkling-type wine, rack the wine off the lees when it has a gravity of 1010 and fine with Bentonite, or any other proprietary brand of finings. As soon as the wine clears siphon into champagne bottles. Stopper with plastic champagne stoppers and wire down. Do *not* prime the bottles with sugar as there will be sufficient unconverted sugar in the wine to produce the secondary fermentation. *Do not use bottles other than genuine champagne bottles for sparkling wines.*

Gorse flower wine

Gorse bushes are found growing on heaths and wasteland throughout the British Isles. Be sure to gather the flowers on a dry, sunny day as the flower remains closed during damp weather and will harbour many insects.

If you like the hock and Moselle wines, gorse flower wine is an ideal one to make.

GORSE FLOWER WINE

To make 1 gallon (4½ litres) light, table wine

1 pint (6 dl.) fresh gorse flowers or
  1 oz. (25 g.) dried gorse flowers
7 pints (3¾ litres) water
1½ lb. (675 g.) sugar
½ pint (3 dl.) grape concentrate or
  8 oz. (225 g.) sultanas, chopped
¼ teaspoon citric acid
1 teaspoon tartaric acid

¼ teaspoon malic acid
¼ teaspoon tannin
1 teaspoon nutrient salts
¼ teaspoon energiser or 1 3-mg.
  vitamin B1 tablet
pectic enzyme (if using sultanas)
general purpose yeast

Put the flowers in a sterilised 2-gallon (9-litre) polythene pail and cover with boiling water. Leave to infuse for 15–20 minutes, then strain off the extract into a second sterilised pail. Add the sugar and stir until dissolved. Add the grape concentrate or sultanas plus the remaining ingredients – add the pectic enzyme (if used) and yeast according to the manufacturer's instructions. Cover the pail with a lid or a clean tea towel and leave in a warm place (about 75°F., 24°C.) to ferment, stirring once a day for the first 3 days.

After 3 days, transfer the fermenting liquid into a 1-gallon (4½-litre) jar (or other suitable container). If necessary, top the jar up with cooled, boiled water. If heavy frothing occurs after you have transferred the liquid to the jar, allow it to subside before topping up. Fit the air lock and return the jar to the warm place for further fermentation.

After 14 days from the start, check the gravity with the hydrometer (or by tasting). If the wine has a gravity of 1000 (or is dry to taste), then the wine has achieved its alcohol potential. To allow the wine to ferment any further only reduces the balance which will create problems later on.

Rack the wine off the lees into a sterilised jar, add 2 crushed Campden tablets and leave for 48 hours. Filter the wine to remove any debris which may give it off-flavours. After filtering, adjust the wine to suit the palate. If acidic adjustment is necessary, add 2 or 3 drops of lactic acid.

To make a *social wine*, use 2 pints (generous litre) fresh gorse flowers or 2 oz. (50 g.) dried flowers, 2 lb. (1 kg.) sugar and 1 pint (6 dl.) grape concentrate or 1 lb. (450 g.) chopped sultanas.

Cowslip wine

Cowslips are common, wild flowers found in woods, pasture land, etc. in all parts of the British Isles. Cowslips can be used fresh or in the dried form; only the yellow petals should be used. Do not include any green portion as this can impart a bitterness to the finished wine. Cowslips produce a Sauternes-type wine.

COWSLIP WINE

To make 1 gallon (4½ litres) light, table wine

2 pints (generous litre) fresh cowslip flowers or 1 oz. (25 g.) dried cowslip flowers
7 pints (3¾ litres) water
1½ lb. (675 g.) sugar
½ pint (3 dl.) white grape concentrate or 8 oz. (225 g.) sultanas
1 teaspoon citric acid

½ teaspoon tartaric acid
1 teaspoon nutrient salts or 1 nutrient tablet
¼ teaspoon tannin
¼ teaspoon energiser or 1 3-mg. vitamin B1 tablet
pectic enzyme (if using sultanas)
general purpose yeast

Put the flowers in a sterilised 2-gallon (9-litre) polythene pail and cover with boiling water. Leave to infuse for 15–20 minutes, then strain off the extract into a second sterilised pail. Add the sugar and stir until dissolved. Add the grape concentrate or sultanas plus the remaining ingredients – add the pectic enzyme (if used) and yeast according to the manufacturer's instructions. Cover the pail with a lid or a clean tea towel, and leave in a warm place (about 75°F., 24°C.) to ferment, stirring once a day for the first 3 days.

After 3 days, transfer the fermenting liquid into a 1-gallon (4½-litre) jar (or other suitable container). If necessary, top the jar up with cooled, boiled water. If heavy frothing occurs after you have transferred the liquid to the jar allow it to subside before topping up. Fit the air lock and return the jar to the warm place for further fermentation.

After 14 days from the start, check the gravity with the hydrometer (or by tasting). If the wine has a gravity of 1000 (or is dry to taste), then the wine has achieved its alcohol potential. To allow the wine to ferment any further only reduces the balance which will create problems later on.

Rack the wine off the lees into a sterilised jar, add 2 crushed Campden tablets and leave for 48 hours. Filter the wine to remove any debris which may give it off-flavours. After filtering, adjust the wine to suit the palate. If acidic adjustment is necessary, add 2 or 3 drops of lactic acid.

To make a *social wine*, use 3 pints (1½ litres) fresh cowslip flowers or 2 oz. (50 g.) dried cowslip flowers, 2 lb. (1 kg.) sugar and 1 pint (6 dl.) white grape concentrate or 1 lb. (450 g.) sultanas.

Lime flower wine

The lime flower is also known as the linden flower and has quite a reputation for its tonic properties, so with a gallon or two of lime flower wine in your store you would be able to take a tonic in the most pleasant and appealing manner.

Do *not* over-steep the flowers and bracts during the infusion process otherwise the flavour becomes overpowering and destroys the delicacy of a potentially enjoyable, light wine. It should be served chilled in a large glass with 1 or 2 ice cubes and a sprig of mint added.

LIME FLOWER WINE

To make 1 gallon (4½ litres) light, social wine

1 oz. (25 g.) dried lime flowers
7 pints (3¾ litres) water
1½ lb. (675 g.) sugar
8 oz. (225 g.) raisins or sultanas, or
 ½ pint (3 dl.) white grape
 concentrate
1 teaspoon citric acid
½ teaspoon tartaric acid

1 teaspoon nutrient salts
¼ teaspoon energiser or 1 3-mg.
 vitamin B1 tablet
¼ teaspoon tannin
pectic enzyme (if using raisins or
 sultanas)
general purpose yeast

Put the flowers in a sterilised 2-gallon (9-litre) polythene pail and cover with boiling water. Leave to infuse for 15–20 minutes, then strain off the extract into a second sterilised pail. Add the sugar and stir until dissolved. Add the raisins or sultanas, or grape concentrate plus the remaining ingredients – add the pectic enzyme (if used) and yeast according to the manufacturer's instructions. Cover the pail with a lid or a clean tea towel and leave in a warm place (about 75°F., 24°C.) to ferment, stirring once a day for the first 3 days.

After 3 days, transfer the fermenting liquid into a 1-gallon (4½-litre) jar (or other suitable container). If necessary, top the jar up with cooled, boiled water. If heavy frothing occurs after you have transferred the liquid to the jar allow it to subside before topping up. Fit the air lock and return the jar to the warm place for further fermentation.

After 14 days from the start, check the gravity with the hydrometer (or by tasting). If the wine has a gravity of 1000 (or is dry to taste), then the wine has achieved its alcohol potential. To allow the wine to ferment any further only reduces the balance which will create problems later on.

Rack the wine off the lees into a sterilised jar, add 2 crushed Campden tablets and leave for 48 hours. Filter the wine to remove any debris which may give it off-flavours. After filtering, adjust the wine to suit the palate. If acidic adjustment is necessary, add 2 or 3 drops of lactic acid.

Sparkling-type wine

To produce a sparkling-type wine, rack the wine off the lees when it has a gravity of 1010 and fine with Bentonite, or any other proprietary brand of finings. As soon as the wine clears, siphon into champagne bottles, stopper with plastic champagne stoppers and wire down. Do *not* prime the bottles with sugar as there will be sufficient unconverted sugar in the wine to produce the secondary fermentation. *Do not use bottles other than genuine champagne bottles for sparkling wines.*

PRIMROSE WINE

To make 1 gallon (4½ litres)

2 pints (generous litre) primroses
7 pints (3¾ litres) water
2 lb. (1 kg.) sugar
½ pint (3 dl.) white grape concentrate

1½ teaspoons citric acid
1 teaspoon yeast nutrient
¼ teaspoon grape tannin
general purpose yeast

Put the flowers in a sterilised 2-gallon (9-litre) polythene pail and cover with the boiling water. Leave to infuse for 15–20 minutes, then strain off the extract into a second sterilised pail. Add the sugar and stir until dissolved. Add the grape concentrate and the remaining ingredients – add the yeast according to the manufacturer's instructions. Cover the pail with a lid or a clean tea towel and leave in a warm place (about 75°F., 24°C.) to ferment, stirring once a day for the first 3 days.

After 3 days, transfer the fermenting liquid into a 1-gallon (4½-litre) jar (or other suitable container). If necessary, top the jar up with cooled, boiled water. If heavy frothing occurs after you have transferred the liquid to the jar allow it to subside before topping up. Fit the air lock and return the jar to the warm place for further fermentation.

After 14 days from the start, check the gravity with the hydrometer (or by tasting). If the wine has a gravity of 1000 (or is dry to taste), then the wine has achieved its alcohol potential. To allow the wine to ferment any further only reduces the balance which will create problems later on.

Rack the wine off the lees into a sterilised jar, add 2 crushed Campden tablets and leave for 48 hours. Filter the wine to remove any debris which may give it off-flavours. After filtering, adjust the wine to suit the palate. If acidic adjustment is necessary, add 2 or 3 drops of lactic acid.

Mead

Mead is possibly one of the oldest alcoholic drinks known to man. Even with no wine making knowledge one can produce an alcoholic beverage simply by diluting honey with water and allowing natural fermentation to take place.

The quality, potency and longevity of the resultant exercise would however be unpredictable and the purpose of this section is to present recipes which control and assure that the end product will be worthy of praise.

The only difference between mead and wine is in the variable section of the basic recipe, bearing in mind that in a true mead sugar is not used. However, the variations on the theme as given in the following recipes are well worth trying. We have tried the recipes, the experts have tasted them and awarded them the highest honours. What better proof of qualities attainable, and incentive to experiment? Before starting on the recipes let us describe some of the honeys, then it becomes your prerogative to use the honey of your choice.

Heather honey Dark and strongly-flavoured and highly recommended as a blend to give bouquet, colour and all the basic attributes expected of mead.

Clover honey Light in colour and quite mild.

Lime honey Very pale amber with a greenish tinge and distinctive flavour.

Acacia honey Light with a delicate bouquet and matching flavour.

Apple blossom Light in colour with a delicate flavour and good bouquet.

Orange blossom Pale with a delicate flavour and equally delicate bouquet.

Leatherwood Pale in colour but overpowering in bouquet and flavour and should be used sparingly. Reminiscent of elderflower.

Honey-based wines and meads

Mead Based purely on honey.

Pyment Grape wines sweetened with honey.

Cyser Apple wine with honey used either as the sweetening agent or as part of fermentable sugar content in the must.

Melomel Honey fermented with any other fruit juice, other than apple or grape.

Metheglin Any of the above with the addition of herbs or spices.

MEAD

To make 1 gallon (4½ litres) full-bodied mead

4 lb. (2 kg.) honey (flavour and colour
  will depend on type used)
1 teaspoon citric acid
½ teaspoon tartaric acid
¼ teaspoon tannin

1 teaspoon nutrient
¼ teaspoon energiser or 1 3-mg.
  vitamin B1 tablet
general purpose yeast

Dissolve the honey in a sterilised polythene pail with sufficient boiling water to make up to 1 gallon (4½ litres). Allow to cool to about 65–70°F. (17–21°C.), then add the remainder of the ingredients, stirring well to dissolve them. (Add the yeast according to the manufacturer's instructions.) Cover the pail with a lid or clean tea towel and leave to stand in a warm place (70–75°F., 21–24°C.) to ferment, stirring daily for the first 3–4 days to dispel the carbon dioxide and to encourage a good yeast development.

After 7 days from the start, transfer the fermenting liquid to a 1-gallon (4½-litre) jar and fit the air lock. Return the jar to the warm place and allow to ferment until the gravity of the mead drops to 1000. Rack off into a second sterilised 1-gallon (4½-litre) jar and add 2 crushed Campden tablets. After 48 hours, filter to remove the solids and to polish the mead. The mead can now be adjusted for early drinking, or stored for further maturing if desired. It is advisable to store in bulk for at least 3 months prior to bottling if you intend to bottle and bin for future use.

A lighter-bodied mead can be produced by simply reducing the honey by 1 lb. (450 g.).

It is recommended that full-bodied meads be treated as dessert or social wines.

We also suggest that you make 3 or 4 gallons (13½ or 18 litres) of mead based on this recipe, but using the various honeys given opposite.

WHITE PYMENT

To make 1 gallon (4½ litres) medium-bodied, table wine

1½ lb. (675 g.) light-coloured honey
1 pint (6 dl.) white grape concentrate
1 teaspoon citric acid
1 teaspoon nutrient salts

¼ teaspoon tannin
¼ teaspoon energiser or 1 3-mg.
  vitamin B1 tablet
general purpose yeast

Follow the same method as for making mead (see opposite).

Excellent results can also be obtained by using any one of the following honeys:

Acacia   Apple blossom
Lime   Clover

The red variety of pyment can be made from this recipe by using red grape concentrate instead of white, or the rosé version by using a rosé concentrate.

CYSER

To make 1 gallon (4½ litres) table wine

5–7 lb. (2½–3½ kg.) apples (half cooking apples and half eating apples) or 1 pint (6 dl.) apple concentrate

2½ lb. (1¼ kg.) apple blossom or acacia honey

4 pints (2¼ litres) boiling water

1 teaspoon citric acid
1 teaspoon nutrient salts
¼ teaspoon tannin
pectic enzyme
¼ teaspoon energiser or 1 3-mg. vitamin B1 tablet
general purpose yeast

Wash and core the apples (leave the peel on to retain the tannin), then chop roughly and put into a clean sterilised polythene pail (marked up to the 1-gallon/4½-litre level). Dissolve the honey in the boiling water and pour over the prepared apples (or apple juice). Make up to 1 gallon (4½ litres) with cold water then add the remaining ingredients. Cover with a lid or a clean tea towel and leave to stand in a warm place (70–75°F., 21–24°C.) to ferment, stirring daily for the first 3 or 4 days. Strain the liquid off the pulp into a sterilised 1-gallon (4½-litre) jar and fit the air lock. (Do not press out the pulp otherwise unwanted gums, pectins and fine pulp matter can create problems at a later stage.) Return the fermenting vessel to the warm place for further fermentation until the gravity drops to 1000. Rack into a second sterilised jar and add 2 crushed Campden tablets. After 48 hours, filter and adjust for acidic and sugar balance to suit the palate.

To make a *social wine*, use 7–10 lb. (3½–4½ kg.) apples or 1 pint (6 dl.) apple concentrate and 3 lb. (1½ kg.) apple blossom or acacia honey.

Melomel

It is not necessary to give individual recipes for melomel as any of the fruit-based wine recipes may be used simply by substituting honey for the sugar. However, a few recommendations and some advice will be helpful.

Recommended fruit-based wines

Light melomel (white) Gooseberries, golden plums, fresh apricots, quinces, pears

Light melomel (rosé) Raspberries, loganberries, redcurrants, red plums

Light melomel (red) Blackberries, elderberries, bilberries, damsons, blackcurrants

For the white and rosé melomels use either apple blossom or acacia honey; for the red melomel use either heather or clover honey.

For light wines use $2\frac{1}{2}$ lb. ($1\frac{1}{8}$ kg.) of honey per gallon ($4\frac{1}{2}$ litres).

For medium wines use 3 lb. ($1\frac{1}{2}$ kg.) of honey per gallon ($4\frac{1}{2}$ litres).

For social or dessert wines use $3\frac{1}{2}$ lb. ($1\frac{3}{4}$ kg.) and $4\frac{1}{2}$ lb. ($2\frac{1}{4}$ kg.) of honey per gallon ($4\frac{1}{2}$ litres), respectively.

Use the fruit quantities as recommended in the recipes.

Our method of producing melomels is to blend a straight, finished mead and wine together, starting with equal amounts of each and then adjusting, either with the straight wine or the mead until the required balance is reached. This method allows you to produce an instant melomel from any of your fruit-based wines, providing of course you have 1 or 2 gallons ($4\frac{1}{2}$ or 9 litres) of straight mead.

The permutations are endless and the results exciting. The great advantage is that one can produce a bottle of melomel given only a few minutes' notice.

You could also blend a flower-based wine with mead, but use one made with a mild honey, otherwise the delicacy of the balance will be upset.

Metheglin

As with melomel, no special recipes are needed to produce metheglin. Any straight mead with the addition of herbs or spices is classified as a metheglin. Once again one is presented with an exciting experiment. Discovering the various flavours need not be a long, drawn-out process, neither need it be expensive, for 1 gallon ($4\frac{1}{2}$ litres) of mead can give you six bottles of metheglin, each with a different flavour.

Make 1 gallon ($4\frac{1}{2}$ litres) of mead as the recipe on page 54 and when the gravity reaches 1010 siphon the mead from the gallon jar into six wine bottles.

To the first bottle add $\frac{1}{4}$ teaspoon ground ginger
To the second bottle add 6 cloves
To the third bottle add 1 stick cinnamon
To the fourth bottle add 1 sprig mint, well bruised
To the fifth bottle add 1 teaspoon allspice
To the sixth bottle add 1 sprig fennel, well bruised

Plug the necks of the bottles with clean cotton wool and allow the mead to continue fermenting in the bottles for a further 10–12 days, after which time each bottle can be filtered into a standard-size wine bottle. If necessary, top up with some finished mead or wine. You now have a variety of flavours to sample and to discover which you would like to produce in 1-gallon ($4\frac{1}{2}$-litre) quantities.

Fortified wines

Aperitifs

Aperitifs can be produced easily from the basic wine simply by adding dry herbs to the finished fermented wine. Allow them to infuse until the desired flavour strength has been obtained. The wines should then be re-filtered, and fortified with spirit to raise the alcohol level to about 17%.

Aperitifs should be light in texture and sufficiently astringent to activate the taste buds.

Liqueurs

It is possible to produce liqueurs from the basic recipe by the addition of a little glycerine and brandy, to give that extra body which is characteristic of liqueurs.

Avoid the use of vodka or neutral spirits (often recommended in wine making books) as the fortifying medium. It must be appreciated that the origin of most liqueurs is herbs or fruit steeped in brandy, or other appropriate spirit, e.g. the adjustment for a drambuie-type liqueur would be to add whisky, while a cherry brandy-type would be fortified with brandy. Brandy is also used in the production of sherry, port and other fortified wines.

Port

Recipe A good port wine can be made by sweetening a full-bodied, Burgundy-type wine and adding 1 sherry glass of brandy per bottle.
Accompany Cheese and biscuits.
Serve At room temperature (65–70°F., 17–21°C.).
Type of glass A port glass.

Sherry

Recipe A good sherry-type wine can be made from a base of sherry-type concentrate, or from a basic wine made with rose hips and raisins and fortified, after filtering, with 1 sherry glass of brandy per bottle.
Accompany The soup course, or serve as an aperitif or to end the meal.
Serve At a temperature of between 50–60°F. (10–16°C.).
Type of glass A sherry glass.

Fruit cups and punches

On pages 59 and 60 you will see a recipe for a fruit cup and a punch. We have included these because we feel that having made successful wines, following our method, you may want to entertain your friends and serve a fruit cup or a punch.

A fruit cup is ideal to serve in the garden on a summer's day. A punch bowl is just right for serving in the winter, around a glowing fire. A fruit cup begins a party and a punch says 'goodnight'. The acquisition of a punch bowl with a ladle would be a worthwhile investment.

When you want to serve a fruit cup, take out the dividers of the ice tray, pour fresh water into the tray and freeze the water in one solid block. The ice will last much longer in the fruit cup this way because the surfaces subjected to the warmer liquid are fewer, therefore it will take that much longer to melt.

A punch is a very popular drink for, coupled with nutmeg and ginger, the wines are guaranteed to warm the cockles of the heart on a chilly evening. As it is a drink to be served at departure time never use your very best wines for making it. Your guests should have been offered these earlier. But having said that, do not use wines of a sub-standard. Sound, basic wines are necessary to produce good punches and good fruit cups.

The following recipes are based on using the *basic recipe* and facts given in this and earlier chapters. So full comprehension of all the chapters is paramount in the appreciation of the reasons for recipes' ingredient amounts, which may appear at variance with the basic recipe. For example – in the recipe on page 26 for light-bodied, white, table wines (dry) the sugar is shown as 1 lb. 10 oz. (725 g.) to each gallon (4½ litres). In the basic recipe this minimum is given as 2 lb. (1 kg.) per gallon (4½ litres). Why the difference? You will find that explained on pages 16–18 where we mention alcohol content. With fruit cups we feel that 8·6% of alcohol by volume is sufficient for the wine base, as the fruits we recommend you to use will also produce, through a natural sugar content, a certain amount of alcohol. With experience you will arrive at your own conclusions, which is what we have been 'preaching' throughout this book.

To make a fruit cup

With a selection of wines to hand take a large, glass fruit bowl, capable of holding approximately 1 gallon (4½ litres), and a ladle. Place a large block of ice in the bowl and pour in 3 bottles of chilled, white wine – medium-bodied and medium-sweet. Add to this 2 bottles of sparkling, chilled lemonade. Now add 1 thinly sliced, large apple; 1 thinly sliced orange and 1 thinly sliced lemon. The peel from the lemon and orange may be arranged over the edges of the bowl as a decoration. One or two washed roses floated on the surface of the bowl complete the decoration and make the fruit cup look almost too good to drink.

Next to the bowl containing the fruit cup have a glass with sprigs of mint, and a dish of cocktail cherries, some olives and also some washed grapes. A squat-type tumbler is ideal to serve the fruit cup in. Long cocktail forks, made of coloured plastic, can be used to spear either a cherry, olive or grape to place in the glass prior to filling with the fruit cup – an ice cube may also be added to the glass if liked, together with a sprig of mint. Allow $\frac{1}{2}$ pint (3 dl.) of fruit cup per guest.

The colours and flavours of fruit cups can be individually changed to suit your guests simply by using the great variety of flavourings sold by home wine making suppliers. For instance, you could have six glasses of fruit cup from the bowl and end up with one peach-flavoured, one apricot-flavoured, one strawberry-flavoured, one mint-flavoured, one cherry-flavoured and one orange-flavoured. Each one will be the appropriate colour.

To make a punch

For 1 gallon ($4\frac{1}{2}$ litres) of punch, place 4 bottles basic, red, medium wine in a pan. Bring to the boil and add 12 cloves, 3 sticks cinnamon, $\frac{1}{4}$ grated nutmeg and $\frac{1}{2}$ teaspoon ground ginger.

Simmer for 10 minutes, then add 2 bottles of ginger ale and $\frac{1}{8}$ bottle rum or brandy to fortify the punch.

Add 1 sliced orange and serve with green ginger or melon slices.

Other fruits may be added, as liked, but do not use grapefruit as it will over-flavour everything. Allow $\frac{1}{2}$ pint (3 dl.) of punch per guest.

White wine fruit cup

---

3 bottles white wine	1 lemon
1 bottle mead	1 orange
1 bottle sparkling lemonade	1 apple
1 bottle pure apple juice	few sprigs mint
$\frac{1}{4}$ bottle white rum	

Place a piece of ice, about the size of a $\frac{1}{2}$-pint (3-dl.) tumbler, in the punch bowl. Pour the chilled wine, mead, lemonade, apple juice and rum into the bowl. Add the thinly pared lemon and orange peel; then slice the lemon and orange and add the slices. Finally, peel, core and slice the apple and add to the punch bowl. Decorate the punch bowl with sprigs of bruised mint.

JAMAICAN PUNCH

grated rind of 1 orange
2 pints (generous litre) strong tea
  (without milk)
3 bottles dry elderberry or bilberry
  wine

8 oz. (225 g.) soft brown sugar
2 pints (generous litre) cider
½ bottle rum
pinch nutmeg and cinnamon
2 medium oranges, thinly sliced

If using a glass punch bowl put in the cold ingredients first, but if using an earthenware or silver bowl it is not necessary to do this.

Add the grated orange rind to the tea and allow it to infuse for about 7 minutes. Strain the tea into the punch bowl. Heat the wine in a large saucepan or preserving pan, but do not allow it to boil. Add the sugar and stir until dissolved, then pour into the punch bowl. Add the remaining ingredients.

Other spices, such as ginger and cloves, may be added, but it is best to check that your guests like such flavours.

GOLDEN DAWN

3 bottles rose hip wine (made from
  dried hips or shells)
2 bottles ginger ale
1 bottle ginger wine
2 pints (generous litre) pale ale

8 oz. (225 g.) demerara sugar
½ pint (3 dl.) water
½ bottle brandy
2 oranges
1 lemon

For a cold drink, chill the wines and ale before adding them to the punch bowl. Place the sugar and water in a saucepan and stir over a low heat until dissolved. Chill. Put a block of ice, about the size of a ½-pint (3-dl.) tumbler, into the punch bowl. Pour in the chilled ingredients together with the brandy and chilled sugar syrup. Slice the rind thinly from one of the oranges and from the lemon; cut the fruit into thin slices. Add the fruit rinds and slices to the punch bowl. Serve in tall glasses, with ice cubes if liked.

To make a hot punch, follow the method for Jamaican punch (see above) and add spices if desired.

To make successful fruit cups and punches

Use only clean, uncontaminated ice in block form, not crushed.

Do not add too much spirit – you are not dispensing knock-out drops and the 'kick' is of secondary importance.

Remember a fruit cup should be a refreshing, long drink not a fruit cocktail.

Chill the wines and fruit juices before putting them into the punch bowl with the ice, otherwise the ice will melt quickly and dilute the mix.

Do not add too many varieties of fruit to the cup, and use herbs sparingly.

Vocabulary of terms used in wine making

Aerobic fermentation Fermentation carried out in the initial stages, i.e., the first 3–4 days in the pail, when the wine is in contact with air. Initial yeast growth and development is dependent upon free oxygen supply, therefore stirring daily for the first 3–4 days disperses the carbon dioxide build up and allows development of the yeast colony to a critical concentration stage necessary to break down the sugars which results in the production of alcohol.

Anaerobic fermentation The continuation of the fermentation process under an air lock. Being deprived of a free source of oxygen, the yeast has to degrade the sugars in the must to obtain its oxygen supply thereby hastening the process of alcohol production.

Carbon dioxide This is a by-product of the fermentation caused by yeast acting upon the sugars in the wine. It creates a protective blanket over the wine during the fermenting stage and escapes through the air lock, by nature of the pressure created in its production.

Filtering The final clearing of the wine prior to bottling. Filtering ensures that the wine is bottled in a bright and clear condition.

Fining Clearing the wine by adding isinglass or Bentonite.

Lees Deposits of dead yeast cells and pulp debris which accumulate at the bottom of the fermentation vessel during the fermentation period. Heavy deposits should be removed as they provide ideal breeding grounds for bacteria and can be responsible for off-flavours developing at a later stage.

Must The pulp and additives combined in the first stages of wine making, i.e. when a pulp fermentation is under way the mixture is referred to as the must.

Racking Removing the wine off the deposits by means of a siphon tube with an attachment designed to ensure that flow can be regulated to siphon to any required depth.

Terms used in assessing a wine

Astringency Drying of the mouth. If this is caused by excessive tannin it is unpleasant. In moderate proportion it is a desirable constituent of the balance of a wine.

Balance The balance of the wine is the harmonious combination of the desirable elements – alcohol, acid, tannin, flavour.

Bitterness Usually caused through a too long pulp fermentation, or using unripe fruit. Citrus wines are rather prone to this fault through the introduction of pith into the must.

Body Not necessarily the physical thickness or viscosity of a wine, but a well-balanced wine in all its constituents.

Coarse A wine with excessive harshness and imbalance, i.e. a thin wine with excessive tannin and alcohol.

Cloying A heavy, sweet wine with insufficient alcohol, acid and astringency to create balance.

Dry When the total sugar has been converted into alcohol. Gravity of 1000 or lower.

Dumb or flat A wine lacking in the essential, desirable qualities – acid, tannin and alcohol balance.

Green A young wine not given time to allow the marrying up of its constituents.

Harsh A wine with alcohol in excess of the other constituents of the wine. Usually caused by allowing fermentation to proceed beyond the point of sugar conversion.

Insipid A wine lacking in character. Acidic deficiency.

Medium dry A basically dry wine with just a trace of sugar.

Medium sweet A wine which retains its overtone of sweetness on the palate.

Mellow A mature wine in which glycerol development imparts a smoothness.

Mousey A wine with a nose reminiscent of damp, mouldy paper. Caused by bacterial infection and lack of cleanliness in equipment and utensils.

Prickle A tingling sensation on the tongue due to the presence of dissolved carbon dioxide in the wine.

Rich or round A combination of robustness and mellowness.

Robust A term applied to a full-bodied, well-balanced wine.

Soft or bland An out-of-balance, though not unpleasant, wine. Lacking in astringency and acidity.

Tart A wine containing excessive acid, or the rawness of unripe fruit.

Unbalanced A wine lacking in one or more of the essential balancing constituents.